a
journey
of taste

Favorite Recipes from
Mii amo Spa in Sedona

a
journey
of taste

CHRONICLE BOOKS
SAN FRANCISCO

a destination spa at Enchantment

Text copyright © 2008 by Mii amo Spa.
Photographs copyright © 2008 by Rita Maas.
All rights reserved. No part of this book may
be reproduced in any form without written
permission from the publisher.

Text by Babs Harrison.
Design by Design MW.
Recipe editing by Peggy Fallon.

Sriracha is a registered trademark
of Huy Fong Foods.

Library of Congress Cataloging-in-Publication
Data available.

ISBN: 978-0-8118-6549-4

Manufactured in China.

10 9 8 7 6 5 4 3 2 1

Chronicle Books LLC
680 Second Street
San Francisco, California 94107

www.chroniclebooks.com

Contents

/p. 9   Introduction
/p. 15 A Day at the Spa
/p. 23 Recipes

Breakfast

/p. 30 Mii amo Passage Smoothie
/p. 32 Mayan Breeze Smoothie
/p. 34 Berry Temptress Smoothie
/p. 35 Blueberry Muffins
/p. 37 Berry Yogurt Parfait
        with Granola
/p. 39 Apple Cottage Griddle Cakes
/p. 40 Egg White Omelet
/p. 42 Tofu Scramble
/p. 44 Cinnamon French Toast
/p. 47 Blue Corn Waffles
        with Dried Fruit Compote
/p. 50 Carrot-Bran Muffins
/p. 51 Cranberry-Orange Bread

Lunch

/p. 54 Tomato Gazpacho
/p. 56 Asian Chicken Salad with
        Miso-Mango Vinaigrette
/p. 59 Pan-Seared Ahi Tuna with
        Cellophane Noodles and
        Red Curry Broth
/p. 61 Salmon and Spinach Risotto
        with Red Wine Glaze
/p. 65 Crab Spring Rolls with
        Mango-Chile Dipping Sauce
/p. 68 Vegetarian Chili
/p. 71 Chicken Napoleon
        with Cabernet Jus
/p. 73 Veggie Burger with
        Sweet Onion Ketchup
/p. 76 Whole Wheat–Honey Flatbread
        with Prosciutto and
        Three-Herb Pesto

Dinner

- /p. 82 Artichoke Spread
- /p. 83 Tuscan White Bean Spread
- /p. 84 Warm Crab Spread
- /p. 86 Hummus
- /p. 87 Roasted Eggplant and Red Pepper Spread
- /p. 88 Baby Beet Salad with Tart Cherry Vinaigrette
- /p. 91 Arugula and Tomato Salad with Basil Vinaigrette and Balsamic Syrup
- /p. 94 Onion Soup
- /p. 96 Crab and Corn Cakes with Rémoulade Sauce
- /p. 99 Shrimp Sauté with Orzo and Vegetables
- /p. 100 Grilled Salmon with Yukon Gold Potato Tart and Asparagus-Asiago Cream
- /p. 104 Grilled Sea Bass with Orzo Primavera and Saffron Broth
- /p. 107 Herb-Crusted Colorado Lamb with Rosemary Jus
- /p. 110 Filet Mignon with Truffled Peruvian Potatoes and Wild Mushroom Demi-Glace
- /p. 112 Buffalo Tenderloin with Horseradish Potato Cake and Chipotle-Tomato Jus

Dessert

- /p. 118 Berry Martini
- /p. 119 Peach-Blueberry Crisp
- /p. 120 Fresh Fruit Tart
- /p. 122 Cherry-Apple Strudel
- /p. 124 Fruit Sorbet
- /p. 126 Tiramisu
- /p. 128 Tapioca Pudding Brûlée
- /p. 129 Crème Brûlée with Fresh Berries
- /p. 130 Almond Ricotta Torte
- /p. 132 Chocolate Chip Cheesecake

/p. 135 **Suggested Menus**
/p. 140 **Index**
/p. 144 **Table of Equivalents**

Introduction

Stress.
Too much work, too little time.
Burn out.
Where's the relief?

Welcome to Mii amo, a restorative haven tucked amidst the sacred mountains of Sedona, Arizona. Go to rediscover yourself. Go to be you again.

Mii amo, a destination spa for the stressed-out, over-worked, spiritually malnourished souls who seek inner peace and outer glow, opened its doors in January 2001 in Boynton Canyon. Nestled in this sacred canyon, Mii amo (pronounced: me ah'-mo) means "journey," or "one's path" in Yuman, the traditional Native American language of northern Arizona. It also has multilinguistic qualities: In Italian, it means "I love myself" or "indulgence." In Chinese, it sounds like the word for massage. Any way you say it, Mii amo is a place of personal transformation.

A visit to Mii amo is the ultimate journey . . . a release from everyday life to a physically and mentally restorative environment with all the luxuries of a first-class resort. At Mii amo, guests almost always find themselves trying new things—be it new treatments, new ways of thinking about oneself, or perhaps new foods. Old, useless boundaries and limitations evaporate at the front door. It is truly a place for regeneration, a resort that imbues visitors with a new take on life. It's a special place devoted to the healing processes of the physical body, the mind, and the spirit.

Mii amo combines Sedona mystique and age-old Native American wisdom with the backdrop of the astounding beauty of Boynton Canyon. In fact, the Yavapai-Apache consider Boynton Canyon a spiritual place, the site of their creation story. New Age mystics have identified the Boynton Canyon vortex as a site of increased energy rising from the earth, which imparts a sense of euphoria to those around it. Or maybe it's the peacefulness of this beautiful canyon, privately held and pristinely maintained for decades, echoing the sense that you are in a timeless space cradled by four-hundred-foot-high red rock canyon walls beneath a large and sheltering sky. High above, presiding over all, is Kachina Woman, a glorious rock formation that sits at the mouth of Boynton Canyon. Guests at Mii amo know that throughout their stay, Kachina Woman is watching over them and their spiritual-mental-emotional progress.

Long before Mii amo was named the number one destination spa in the world by the readers of *Travel + Leisure* magazine, there was, and still is, Enchantment Resort, Sedona's premier getaway. For more than twenty years, guests have returned time and again to this seventy-acre property in Boynton Canyon. They come for the laid-back and scenic atmosphere, the hiking, biking, and Native American programs for children and adults, and for delicacies like the piñon-crusted rack of lamb, perhaps enjoyed with a robust red wine and even a prickly pear margarita to start.

When Enchantment opened in 1987, the diminutive six-room amenity spa would soon take on a life of its own. Visitors coming to Sedona for spiritual renewal found it at this little spa. It didn't take long to realize there was a need for a completely expanded and enriched spa experience.

The vision was original: This new space would be a separate, intimate spa with fourteen guest rooms and two suites—a destination with its own guest programs—that didn't feel like a traditional spa. It would be a temple for the body, mind, and spirit, perfectly situated in the canyon environment without disrupting the area's natural beauty. And it would be a place where the spa robe would be the common uniform; a spa designed for informality and comfort. This was to be a place where guests would leave behind their baubles, pretenses, and anxieties, where they would come to be as they are, so as to become who they truly want to be. No small order that, but it is exactly what so many of us crave. Mii amo set out to deliver on this tasty promise of personal self-discovery in a gentle, nurturing context.

Gluckman Mayner, the New York–based architecture and interior design firm known for museums and gallery spaces (but not a single spa), took up the challenge. Their projects include the Georgia O'Keeffe Museum in Santa Fe, New Mexico; the Deutsche Guggenheim in Berlin, Germany; the Museo Picasso Málaga in Spain; and the expansion of the Whitney Museum of American Art in New York City. Their sensibility to art and light would prove to be the perfect match for the project.

To create Mii amo, Gluckman Mayner joined modern design with the local vernacular, using their experience of creating spaces for the enjoyment of art to create meditative spaces to define the spa. Natural light and moving water are essential elements throughout. Each window frames a view of the canyon finer than any painting. The structure is minimalist with strong, clean lines, yet feels integrally woven into the tapestry of this preternatural canyon.

Nineteen treatment rooms are housed in five adobe brick towers inspired by the Anasazi concept of stacked architecture, and they have the best views. Outdoor treatments are done in four *wikiups*, renditions of Native American structures using rustic wood *latillas*; a Watsu pool is tucked into the hillside.

Guest casitas encircle an inner courtyard. Each has a deep soaking tub and enclosed patio designed for maximum privacy. The Mii amo Luxury Suite features an outdoor fireplace with plunge pool and Jacuzzi, and a massage treatment room.

And then there is the Crystal Grotto. Because Sedona is known as a source of healing crystals, they became a defining, distinctive element of Mii amo. Housed behind the only curve in the otherwise linear building, the Crystal Grotto is the soul of the spa, accentuating the relationship between earth and sky. Inspired by the traditional Native American kiva, a place of ceremony and transformation, the circular room has an earthen floor, an aperture in the domed ceiling, a center fountain, and a crystal mandala made of petrified Arizona pine with a quartz cluster crystal. It also features four large crystals placed in niches around the room to designate the four corners of the world: red vanadinite for east, black obsidian for west, white selenite for north, and yellow citrine for south. The elements of fire, water, earth, and air blend with the crystals for energy and balance.

The Crystal Grotto is used primarily for meditation and crystal sound therapy. It is also where staff and guests gather each morning to set their intentions for the day. Each year on the summer solstice, the sun passes directly over the aperture, which focuses the sun's rays on the quartz crystal in the center. It marks one of four seasonal celebrations at Mii amo.

Connected by a land bridge but separated by a grove of old cottonwood trees from Enchantment Resort, the spa operates as its own entity. Each spa guest is on a customized three-, four-, or seven-night spa program (or longer) that includes treatments, classes, and three meals daily in Mii amo Café. Each guest's program is arranged prior to arrival so they don't have to worry about booking treatments or activities once they are here, leaving them free to focus on a particular goal or intention. Guests from Enchantment Resort also use the spa by day.

At Mii amo, there's at once a sense of community and exclusivity. Arrivals are scheduled on Thursdays and Sundays so a group can move through a spa program together and find support in others. Highly trained therapists, many of whom have been with Mii amo from the beginning, are beloved by guests as wise souls who help them along their path. The intimate nature of the spa allows guests to talk easily with staff.

There's a communal table in the café for those who want to mingle. But for guests who prefer privacy and solitude, it is there for the taking.

And last, but certainly not least, Mii amo's food is not typical spa cuisine. Certainly it is healthful and low fat, but it is also fresh and light and there is no feeling of deprivation. This is food that tantalizes the taste buds while staying in alignment with Mii amo's overarching goals of promoting health and well-being. Is it low-calorie food? For guests who want that, yes. For other guests, it need not be. This is not food that is prescriptive; it is instead a cuisine that celebrates the many choices that are life. This is cuisine for living.

Mii amo's food is not typical spa cuisine. There is no feeling of deprivation. This is food that tantalizes the taste buds while staying in alignment with Mii amo's overarching goals of promoting health and well-being.

In this book, we bring you a taste of the Mii amo lifestyle through recipes for healthy dining, with menus that suggest ways to pair the recipes and tips from the chef on how to add flavor, rather than fat, to your meals. You'll find low-fat, low-cholesterol, and low-carbohydrate selections prepared with a variety of culinary techniques. At Mii amo, we use the highest-quality products available—organically grown fruits and vegetables, quality meats, seafood, and free-range poultry—and that is key to great flavor.

Thank you to our guests, who have requested recipes so many times. This book will keep you on the path until you return to Mii amo. And for those of you who have not yet been here, join us on a journey of Mii amo through these pages.

Look out the windows at Mii amo and you know you are in a special place—but during your stay it is *your* special place.

Each guest's journey is individually designed. No stay is the same as another. Here is one guest's memories of a day in the life of Mii amo.

A day at the spa

I awake early and open the door to find juice and the morning paper. Drink the juice, but leave the pandemonium of the world's news behind to hike Boynton Canyon.

My room key opens the gate just behind the spa and leads me into the Secret Mountain Wilderness where I hike—slowly, but with confidence—up the canyon trail to Kachina Woman. She is thought to be the guardian of this sacred canyon and is a landmark, a stone monolith that many say resembles an Indian maiden with hair blown back. This is the Garden of Eden for the Yavapai tribe: the epicenter of their creation myth, the place where First Woman came to rest after a great flood and, through a sacred ceremony with the sun, the tribe was born. From her base, the view beyond the canyon reaches for miles, and I watch the sun pop up, illuminating the canyon walls with a golden glow. A soft breeze blows, and a sense of renewal washes over me. The silence here is immense, beckoning. I am discovering the sweet gift of focus, of being present in the moment and forgetting everything else.

I head back to Mii amo along the juniper-lined trail to catch the Morning Ritual in the Crystal Grotto. The circle is a symbol of the divine, of wholeness, and as I step in the circular room, I am asked to walk clockwise around the circle to the last seat. Before I sit, I feel the power of Mother Earth supporting me; I take several deep breaths and relax my shoulders.

A therapist asks the seven of us to focus on the center quartz crystal and to set our intention for the day. We may share them aloud and all do as we go around the circle. One by one, there are intentions to be joyful, grateful, to stress less, to be open to love, to relax. We close our eyes and meditate on this as a therapist smudges each of us—wafting a bundle of burning dried sage leaves around us and sounding the crystal bowl over our heads to purify our auras. I feel like I have a mission for the day, one that has been voiced aloud for others to hear, and now I have an obligation to be mindful about achieving it. We are in this together.

On to breakfast at Mii amo Café. The windows perfectly frame a view of the canyon where I was earlier today, a totally different perspective from my perch at the base of Kachina Woman. The menu has so many breakfast choices, I am glad I'm here for a while to try them all. The hike has made me hungry and I order a Berry Temptress Smoothie to start followed by a blue corn waffle. How many calories are in this feast? I check the menu and see that it's just over 300. At home in the city, I might have skipped breakfast (too many calories, not enough time) but here at Mii amo I know I will need the energy for the day ahead of me.

As I eat the waffle—blue corn makes for a terrific and distinctive crunch that transcends ordinary white flour confections—I watch the activity in the open kitchen, where stockpots are already simmering something fragrant for lunch. Later in my stay, the chef will tell me that long-simmering, which produces concentrated, intense flavors, is a secret to the healthy, reduced-fat, and reduced-calorie cuisine that is Mii amo's. There is a method to this culinary artistry.

After breakfast, my first treatment today is a Crystal Bath. I shower and change into a thick spa robe in the locker room and head upstairs to the waiting area. My therapist calls me and shakes my hand, leading me back to a room with an expansive view of the red rock canyon.

As I lie on the table, the therapist anoints each of my seven *chakras*, or energy centers, with essential oils and recites an affirmation over each, laying a different crystal on each chakra. With eyes closed, I am imagining a rainbow of light inside my body as I travel inward, releasing the white noise of my mind. Next I go into the hydrotherapy tub, along with the crystals that are to help magnify the affirmations and my intention, as jets massage different points of my body. My therapist talks to me as I am luxuriating in this giant tub, offering small pieces of wisdom as the treatment continues. Life becomes simple if we know how to handle the challenges, she says. I gaze out onto the canyon as I soak, alone with the crystals for twenty minutes.

Long-simmering, which produces concentrated, intense flavors, is the secret to the healthy cuisine that is Mii amo's. There's a method to this culinary artistry.

My next treatment is an Aura Soma reading. I begin by choosing four crystal bottles out of the one hundred presented to me; each contains two vibrant colors made from herbs, essential oils, gems, and crystals, and represents different life forces and directions. The order in which I choose them reveals something about me, and the therapist proceeds to give me an in-depth reading on what it all means. Color is a gentle vibration, she explains, and it has the power to access our deepest desires and alter our moods. In fact, she says, it can access my very essence. Talk about message in a bottle!

The reading is similar to a tarot card reading, only better. She tells my story through the colors I've chosen: my past, present, and my future potential. What she says resonates; I know these things she is telling me are true. They confirm who I really am. The colored pomander oil she suggests I use will

help bring me back into balance to be whom I am meant to be. I can't wait to get started!

Then I catch the late-morning yoga class. The instructor gives me simple stretches I can do at home to help relax my shoulders. I had no idea so much yoga can even be done while sitting in a chair (I can do this at work! Perhaps even on the subway!). The yoga instructor shows me how having the intention (and doing the work of course) can produce results within five minutes. Take that, busy, hectic days!

Time for lunch! I decide to sit out by the pool. The menu is even better than breakfast. I begin with a flatbread with basil pesto, topped with thin slices of sheer prosciutto, tomato, and mozzarella, almost like a pizza with a rich balsamic flavor. My entrée is a couple of crab spring rolls—not deep fried but wrapped in translucent rice paper and filled with crunchy vegetables like snow peas, carrots, and red pepper, with a yummy dipping sauce. I take the time to savor the meal and the beautiful day, and order a fresh fruit tart and tea as I relax in the shade of the rose-covered latilla terrace.

After lunch, I head to another treatment, one of the spa's signature ones: the Sedona Clay Wrap. It begins with a dry brushing of my body that feels so good. The therapist paints on a sweet-smelling warm clay and cocoa mixture, and then wraps me up in blankets and foil for twenty minutes. I feel nurtured and secure in a silver cocoon. After showering off, it's time for a deep massage with oil. My skin is soft as kidskin gloves—how will I ever keep it this way? Ask a question and the therapist imparts knowledge.

She tells me I can buy the cocoa mixture in the shop and do it at home once a week. Or I can combine sea salts and olive oil for an at-home scrub. How easy is that? She tells me I could kick it up a notch by buying Dead Sea salts and adding essential oil, which is good for pulling out toxins and also relaxing. And she suggests I rub the essential oil on my feet, massage the reflexology points for the neck (since mine is stiff), and gently rub lavender oil around my forehead and temples to relax my jaw before sleeping (to help relieve grinding my teeth).

I go up to the rooftop relaxation terrace to lounge and soak in the scenery of the canyon walls. With my journal, which I received as a gift on my first night at turndown, I write down the home-scrub recipe and stretching exercises that I want to incorporate into my daily routine back home.

Three o'clock! Time for the cooking class. I want to learn how to make some of this food, which is so good but, they promise, also good for you. What is the secret? Seven of us sit up at the counter overlooking the kitchen to find out. Today's class is on buffalo, something I never would have thought to use before but the chef says it's very low in fat, comparatively low in cholesterol, and high in protein. One secret to buffalo: Be aggressive in seasoning because this is meat that by itself does not have a bold flavor profile. Salt, pepper, maybe a nice squeeze of lime, put some cooking spray on the grill, and then this filet is ready for cooking. The lean meat cooks quickly and is best served medium-rare. The chef tells us buffalo is widely available and usually it's in the fresh meat section, so I'm going to ask my butcher; many stores stock both ground buffalo and buffalo steaks. In sixty minutes I've picked up several tips for cooking lighter, plus this is a recipe hearty enough to serve at a dinner party.

This afternoon's treatment goes a bit deeper. Soul Seeker was developed by senior therapists at Mii amo. The therapist and I speak about what's going on in my life so she can use proper *modalities*, including past-life regression. I select a stone and lie under blankets—she begins her work on each chakra as I breathe deeply, she telling me to release all negative thoughts holding me back and to step into the new part of my life. I feel as if I have been drifting, in a dream, and as if a heavy weight has been lifted. My heart chakra was closed, apparently. "A broken heart is an open heart," she wisely says.

Next I join an informal discussion on interpretation of dreams in front of the fireplace. The therapist asks if any of us have the same dream or object recurring. I offer up a recent dream for the group to study, one which I have not been able to make any sense of, involving cars that, apparently, are driving east across the Pacific Ocean, starting from somewhere I

cannot pinpoint (I live in New York for heaven's sake). She says cars are about moving forward, the ocean is about depth, and the journey represents change. Members of the group add thoughtful comments and point out things as I recount the dream, and by the end it all becomes very clear. Will I start keeping a dream journal?

Listening to the dreams of the others is fun, too. Part of what makes Mii amo so engaging are these opportunities to interact with other guests, to share the growth with them. At a guess I would say two thirds of the guests get involved with others, one third stick to themselves, and either path is perfectly right—I don't feel any pressure. There are no prescriptions here.

Tonight I decide to sit at the communal table to chat with some of the other guests I've seen today. Over pita crisps with a hummus dip and organic wine, we talk about the day. I promise to lead them on a hike to the cliff dwelling tomorrow. I order grilled sea bass with a fragrant saffron broth . . . delicious! Hard to believe we can have this many treats, but it is wonderful to feel this good.

One observation I picked up from the cooking class and then saw at meals: Portions at Mii amo are small. For those of us who are spending the day in treatments, small meals based on bold, insightful flavors seem perfectly satisfying. When each bite is a delight, less is more.

Speaking of which, I have one more treatment on the day's schedule. My first-ever Watsu treatment is a silently beautiful mother-and-child water ballet, a form of massage and stretching performed in water. I am spinning in the 98-degree, illuminated, outdoor pool deep inside the sacred canyon, being gently stretched. The therapist is standing in the pool, stalwart as a protective mother. I am cradled in her arms, floating effortlessly, floating on the sound of the night, enraptured by the starry heavens each time I open my eyes. "Relax, let go," she whispers.

I pad off to my casita for bed. The duvet is turned back, the fireplace is aglow, and on my bed is tonight's turndown gift: three small glass jars of fragrant teas and a strainer. Tomorrow I'll attend the Journey of Tea, a class about the health benefits of tea and how to properly steep each one. Flute music is softly playing. The CD is "Moons of Meditation," especially composed for Mii amo by Mockingbird, a local Navajo musician. I am told the beauty of the rocks and ancient cliff dwellings of the Secret Mountain Wilderness, where I hiked this morning, inspired him. The music is a result of his meditations among the rocks. Haunting and mystical, it takes me back to my morning hike. I think of chakras opened, my intention, and ask Spirit Wind to take me there.

I reflect on the things the therapists have taught me today. Life is good. Bad things happen, but I can decide how I will react. Engage in life, work fully, and release fully. I place the string of ghost beads I received on arrival, a delicate necklace of tiny seeds and beads strung by the Hopi, over my journal.

As I collapse into the feather bed, I am tired but also peaceful; my mind is clear and I feel nurtured. The winds begin to blow and become the flute music, taking me up to the canyons to dream as I fall into a sound sleep.

Portions at Mii amo are small. For those of us who are spending the day in treatments, small meals based on bold, insightful flavors seem perfectly satisfying. When each bite is a delight, less is more.

Recipes

A skylight runs the length of the main building at Mii amo, allowing the Arizona sun to illuminate the 172-foot gallery that leads to Mii amo Café. Natural light—the sun—is the source of life.

That is what the skylight provides Mii amo and, in turn, in its own way, Mii amo Café hopes to give its diners food that inspires, that energizes, that helps guests see the new possibilities that indeed surround them.

An open kitchen is the heart of Mii amo Café. There are no secrets here: What you see is what you eat. A communal table and tall chairs are directly in front of the kitchen, allowing guests to watch the action. Daily cooking classes offer an opportunity for guests to find out more about our food and how they can prepare it at home. They learn simple recipes and techniques, and many of those tips are included here.

To live well you must eat well, and that is at the center of how Mii amo nourishes guests. Not only do you look, feel, and think better when fueled by the right foods, but you have the energy to incorporate more movement into your daily routine, which is key to a healthy, stress-free, and balanced life. Spa guests choose from myriad activities every day, including hiking, mountain biking, swimming, tennis, yoga, tai chi, and qigong. They have to be well fueled!

For many guests, what they most remember about a Mii amo stay is the food. Most guests can't believe they are eating spa food, and that's just the point. Mii amo Café changes the paradigm about healthy food. It is light and healthful, but good tasting. Delicious food feeds not just the body, but the soul.

At Mii amo, it's all about the taste. Call this the new-style twenty-first-century bistro. Mii amo offers a fine dining experience that artfully recreates classical, contemporary, and regional flavors while reducing unnecessary fat and calories. Bold, fresh flavors abound. Is this "spa food?" Indeed, it certainly is at Mii amo, but the paradox—one that unravels with every delicious bite—is that Mii amo cuisine is miles away from the proverbial spa meal of tofu with some ground nuts on a bed of sprouts. The tastes at Mii amo delight, excite, and even pamper diners, and what they experience is a contemporary haute cuisine that is food for life.

Central to the Mii amo culinary philosophy is that food should look beautiful as well as taste fantastic. Because food has such an effect on how we look and feel, meals at Mii amo are attractively presented in a serene environment. Guests are invited to set aside time to enjoy their meals, be it in the company of others, or delivered to their room to be savored in front of the fire after a late-night treatment. They learn that good food, eaten mindfully as opposed to on the run, is one of the pleasures of life.

One important lesson learned from the Mii amo kitchens: Know where your food is from. Sourcing is crucial. High-quality ingredients can be used in smaller measures because their taste carries culinary weight. Local sourcing is not always easy in Arizona's foothills, but chefs at Mii amo nonetheless buy local when possible, and when their reach is farther, they insist on only the freshest ingredients: a lobster harvested in Maine yesterday can be on a plate in Sedona today, thanks to overnight delivery.

Another lesson learned: Moderation plays a big role in healthy spa food. Cream and fat—large players in many ordinary restaurants—weigh us down, literally and figuratively. As we arise from a typical restaurant table, we feel heavy. Think about a rack of lamb, slathered in butter—now see Mii amo lamb that is roasted, its flavors enhanced with the right seasonal herbs. No butter added. You already know which one is better for you, but you may be surprised to find out that the Mii amo lamb is so much more flavorful and satisfying.

Is cooking spa-style hard? Let's ask a different question: Is a tasty béchamel sauce easy to make? Old-style cooking relied for much of its flavor on long, laborious cooking techniques, enlivened with prodigious additions of butter, cream, and the rest of the "fat is flavor" culinary philosophy. We no longer need to eat that way (and probably we shouldn't!). Traditional cooking techniques were created before the advent of refrigeration, when strong sauces disguised questionable meat and scarcity demanded cooks make use of just about every part of the cow, pig, or chicken. Nowadays we have freshness on our side and we also can focus on the cuts of meat and fish that produce the most flavor with the least fat. Chew on just that insight and you are digesting one of the big underlying secrets of spa cuisine: It oftentimes is very easy to create.

Each menu item includes full nutritional analysis so guests are aware of what they are consuming, and there are notes on portion size. The menus offer choices for each meal—starters, main courses, and even desserts for lunch and dinner. Guests concerned with weight management are guided in their choices, while other guests select at will.

There is a wine list featuring organic and biodynamic wines to complement the food, to be enjoyed in moderation as an optional enhancement to a meal at the guests' discretion. Mii amo was never intended to be a boot camp, but a place where guests could discover themselves, at their own pace. If a glass of wine is what you want, then enjoy it, metabolize, and move on.

In your hands you hold the manual for living the Mii amo lifestyle. The recipes gathered here are just some of the many favorites Mii amo guests have enjoyed and requested over the years. In the pages that follow, you will also find menu suggestions that offer tips on how to combine the recipes into satisfying meals.

Living well starts at the table and this book is your fast start on living the Mii amo way. As the Yuman say, "Hah Nae Goe Si Mah" (Eat Well).

Join the Journey of Tea

Used to be, tea was simple. It was black, from India, and what more did we need to know? However, we want to know more today; thus Mii amo's "Journey of Tea," an informative, guided tasting that introduces guests to the health benefits of true teas and tealike beverages, and their proper preparation. Real tea is made from the *Camellia sinensis* plant, the source of phytonutrients that are responsible for the health benefits of tea. Some medical studies have claimed tea to be an aid in relieving arthritis pain, boosting the immune system, fighting viruses, and detoxifying the body. But this class is not all science, not hardly.

Guests taste six to eight teas and detect the flavor differences among green, black, and white teas and rooibos. Honey, raw sugar, and citrus slices are provided so they can adjust the flavoring to their liking. Mii amo has several teas blended especially for the spa:

» White Cloud: made from rare and exotic white tea leaves, laced with toasted coconut and sweet pineapple. Naturally low in caffeine.

» Sedona Sun: this luscious blend contains whole cranberries, elderberries, black currants, and "rooibos red." Rooibos, made from the South African "red bush," is a caffeine-free herbal agent high in antioxidants and minerals. Naturally caffeine free.

» Desert Passion: an energizing blend of green tea, Siberian ginseng, marigold flowers, and passion fruit essence. Naturally low in caffeine.

» Kachina Moon: this beautiful tea combines orange and lemon peels, apple pieces, hibiscus, sunflower and rose petals, lavender flowers, black currants, and natural grape essence. Naturally caffeine free.

Breakfast

mii amo passage smoothie

Makes about 1½ cups, to serve 1

Our kitchen is blessed with an abundance of ripe fruits and vegetables throughout the year. In your home kitchen, try freezing small portions of fruit purees to keep on hand for smoothies. Feel free to substitute other seasonal fruits for those listed, or use frozen if need be.

In a blender or food processor, combine the banana, strawberries, ice, apple juice, orange juice, passion fruit puree, and mango puree. Process until frothy and well blended, scraping down the sides of the work bowl as needed. Pour into a large chilled glass and serve at once.

186 cal, 0.5 g fat, 2 g prot, 47 g carb

1	small ripe banana, cut into pieces
6	fresh strawberries, hulled and halved
½	cup ice cubes
1	tablespoon apple juice
1	tablespoon orange juice
1	tablespoon passion fruit puree or juice
1	tablespoon mango puree

mayan breeze smoothie

Makes 1½ cups, to serve 1

We flavor this smoothie with 1 tablespoon of our own house-made coconut puree, but a bit of canned, unsweetened coconut milk—or ½ teaspoon of pure coconut extract—should do the trick at home.

In a blender or food processor, combine the banana, papaya juice, orange juice, ice, blackberries, and coconut milk. Process until frothy and well blended, scraping down the sides of the work bowl as needed. Pour into a large chilled glass and serve at once.

319 cal, 8 g fat, 3 g prot, 64 g carb

1	small ripe banana, cut into pieces
½	cup papaya juice
¼	cup orange juice
¼	cup ice cubes
¼	cup fresh blackberries
2	tablespoons unsweetened coconut milk

berry temptress smoothie

Makes about 1½ cups, to serve 1

The chefs at Mii amo do not routinely add dairy products to smoothies, preferring instead to let the clean, fresh fruit flavors shine through. A small ripe banana provides the requisite creaminess here. This sweet-tart jumble of berries is one of our favorites.

In a blender or food processor, combine the banana, cranberry juice, ice, strawberries, blueberries, blackberries, and raspberries. Process until frothy and well blended, scraping down the sides of the work bowl as needed. Pour into a large chilled glass and serve at once.

216 cal, 1 g fat, 3 g prot, 55 g carb

1	small ripe banana, cut into pieces
½	cup pure cranberry juice or cranberry juice cocktail
½	cup ice cubes
3	fresh strawberries, hulled and halved
¼	cup fresh blueberries
2	tablespoons (about 5) fresh blackberries
2	tablespoons (about 6) fresh raspberries

blueberry muffins

Serves 16

We often vary the fruit in these muffins according to the season, but berries are always a favorite. Whole wheat pastry flour is a fine-textured, soft flour with a high starch content that gives these muffins their tender crumb. Look for it in natural foods stores or in well-stocked supermarkets, either packaged or sold in bulk.

Mix the ingredients until just incorporated. As with any quick bread, if the ingredients are overmixed, they become tough.

Preheat the oven to 350°F. Whisk the flour, baking powder, cardamom, and salt together in a bowl. Finely grind the flax seeds in a spice or coffee grinder and combine them with the water. Mix together the flax seed mixture, soy milk, oil, honey, orange juice, and vanilla. Add the dry ingredients, folding until nearly blended. Fold in the blueberries. Divide the batter evenly among the muffin cups, filling each about two thirds full. Bake until the muffins spring back when touched gently on top and a toothpick inserted into the center comes out clean, about 25 minutes. Transfer the muffins to a wire rack to cool. Serve slightly warm or at room temperature.

210 cal, 8 g fat, 5 g prot, 31 g carb

4½	cups whole wheat flour
1	tablespoon baking powder
1	teaspoon ground cardamom
1	teaspoon kosher salt
½	cup flax seeds
1½	cups water
1	cup regular soy milk
½	cup vegetable or canola oil
½	cup honey
½	cup orange juice
1	tablespoon vanilla extract
1⅓	cups fresh or frozen blueberries

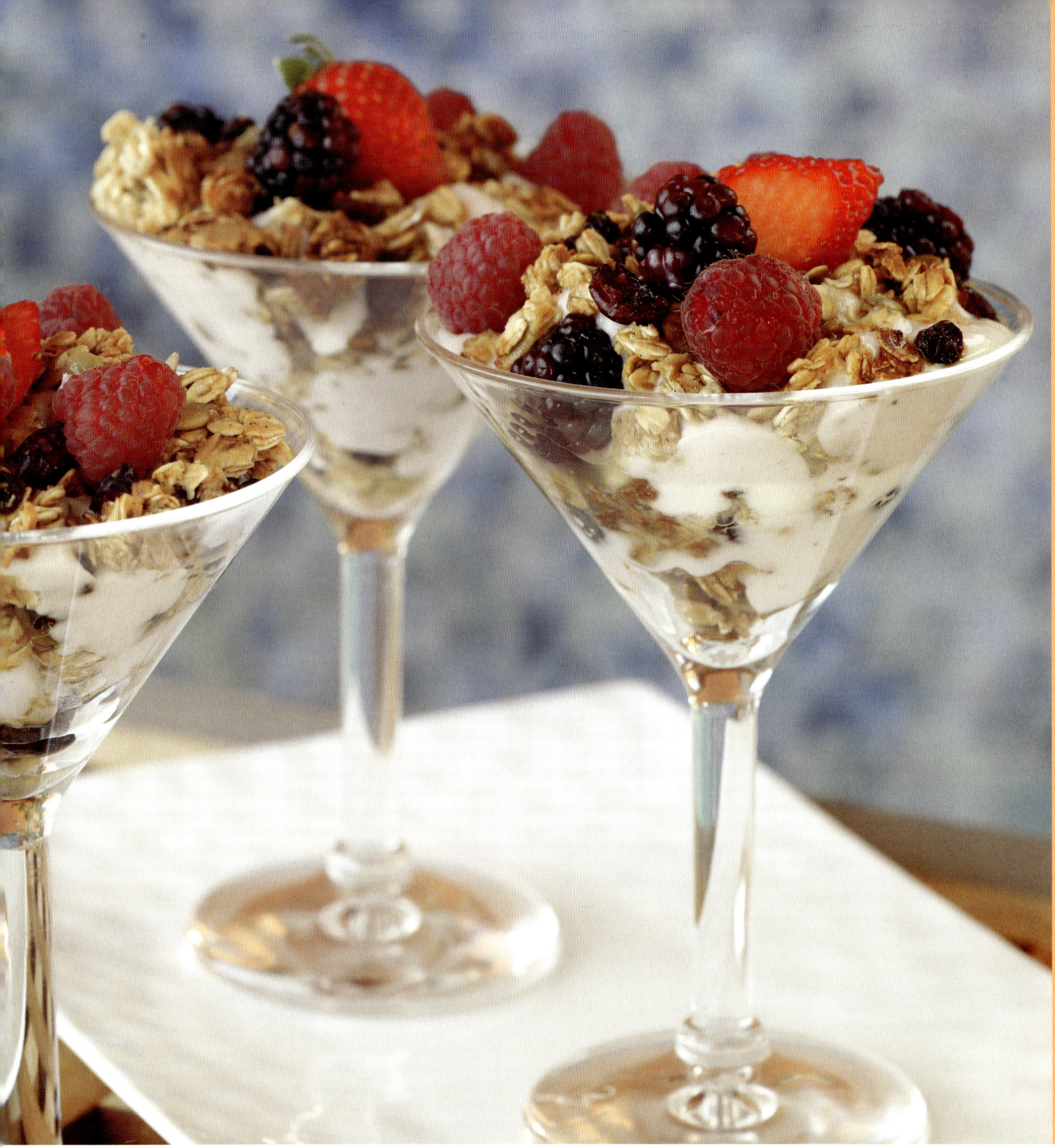

berry yogurt parfait
with granola /p. 38

Serves 4

A whimsical presentation makes this breakfast specialty irresistible, and the hint of spice in our granola complements the intense berry flavors. Vary the berries according to the season, and use whichever are the freshest and most fragrant.

Spoon about 2 tablespoons of yogurt into each of 4 martini glasses. Top the yogurt with about 2 tablespoons of granola and 2 tablespoons berries. Spoon half of the remaining yogurt equally among the 4 glasses and sprinkle with the remaining granola and top with 2 more tablespoons berries. Spoon the remaining yogurt over the top. Mound the remaining berries over the yogurt and garnish each serving with mint. Serve at once.

176 cal, 5 g fat, 7 g prot, 32 g carb

1	cup Granola (recipe follows)
2	cups raspberry or other fruit-flavored nonfat yogurt
2	cups mixed fresh berries, such as strawberries, hulled and quartered, raspberries, and blueberries
4	small fresh mint sprigs, for garnish

granola

Makes about 8 cups, to serve 32

Preheat the oven to 300°F. In a small saucepan, combine the apple juice, vanilla bean or vanilla extract, and cinnamon or ground cinnamon. Cook over medium-high heat until the juice is reduced by half, about 10 minutes. Stir in the honey and bring to a boil. Remove from the heat.

In a large bowl, combine the oats, currants, cranberries, sunflower seeds, and pumpkin seeds. Pour in the apple juice mixture, stirring and tossing until evenly moistened. Spread the mixture into an even layer on a large rimmed baking sheet. Bake, stirring 2 or 3 times, until toasted and fragrant, about 30 minutes. Let cool completely. Use at once, using ¼ cup per serving, or store at room temperature in an airtight container for up to 1 week.

- 2 cups unsweetened apple juice
- 1 vanilla bean, split in half lengthwise, or 1 teaspoon vanilla extract
- 1 (3-inch) cinnamon stick or 1 teaspoon ground cinnamon
- 1 cup honey
- 6 cups old-fashioned rolled oats, such as Quaker Oats
- 1 cup dried currants
- 1 cup dried cranberries
- 1 cup unsalted shelled sunflower seeds
- 1 cup unsalted roasted shelled pumpkin seeds

apple cottage griddle cakes

Serves 5

Shreds of tart apple add moisture as well as flavor to these popular griddle cakes. Serve them warm, drizzled lightly with honey or brown rice syrup, or topped with fresh seasonal fruit.

Preheat an electric or stovetop griddle to about 375°F. In a medium bowl, combine the flour, sugar, baking powder, and salt. Whisk gently to blend.

In a large bowl, whisk together the buttermilk, egg, and egg white until well blended. Stir in the apple and lemon zest. Add the dry ingredients, folding until nearly blended. Fold in the cottage cheese.

Grease the hot griddle with the oil. Working in batches, spoon or ladle ¼-cup portions of the batter onto the griddle, leaving about 2 inches between each griddle cake. Cook for about 3 minutes, or until bubbly and set around the edges. Turn over and cook 2 minutes longer, until cooked through and lightly golden. Keep the cooked griddle cakes warm while you cook the remaining batter. To serve, top as desired and serve warm.

251 cal, 4 g fat, 13 g prot, 45 g carb

1¼	cups all-purpose flour
¼	cup sugar
½	teaspoon baking powder
⅛	teaspoon salt
¼	cup low-fat buttermilk
1	large egg
1	large egg white
1	large tart green apple, such as Granny Smith, peeled, cored, and coarsely grated
1	teaspoon finely grated lemon zest
1	cup low-fat or nonfat cottage cheese
1	teaspoon canola or vegetable oil

egg white omelet

Serves 1

Our omelets are made to order, and that is probably the way you'll want to make them at home, too. For variation, we sometimes add 1½ teaspoons of low-fat cream cheese to the filling. You'll never miss the yolks. When cooking egg, pancake, and French toast items without a griddle, a nonstick skillet works best. Be sure to use heavy-duty plastic utensils so you don't scrape the nonstick coating.

Spray a 7-inch nonstick skillet with nonstick cooking spray. Heat over medium heat until hot but not smoking. Add the spinach, mushroom, green onion, and tomato. Cook, stirring, until the spinach is wilted and the vegetables are heated through, 1 to 2 minutes. Transfer to a small bowl and keep warm.

Wipe the skillet clean with a paper towel and spray again with nonstick cooking spray. Heat over medium heat until hot. Add the egg whites and season with salt and pepper. Use a heatproof rubber spatula to lift up the cooked egg whites from the edges of the pan and let the uncooked white flow beneath, until the omelet is still moist and just set on top, 1½ to 2 minutes. Spread the reserved vegetables down the center, then use the spatula to fold the omelet in half. Transfer it to a warm plate and serve at once.

129 cal, 1 g fat, 20 g prot, 11 g carb

3	tablespoons thinly sliced baby spinach leaves
1	cremini mushroom, thinly sliced
1	tablespoon finely chopped green onion (scallion)
1	tablespoon finely chopped seeded tomato
4	large egg whites

Salt

Freshly ground pepper

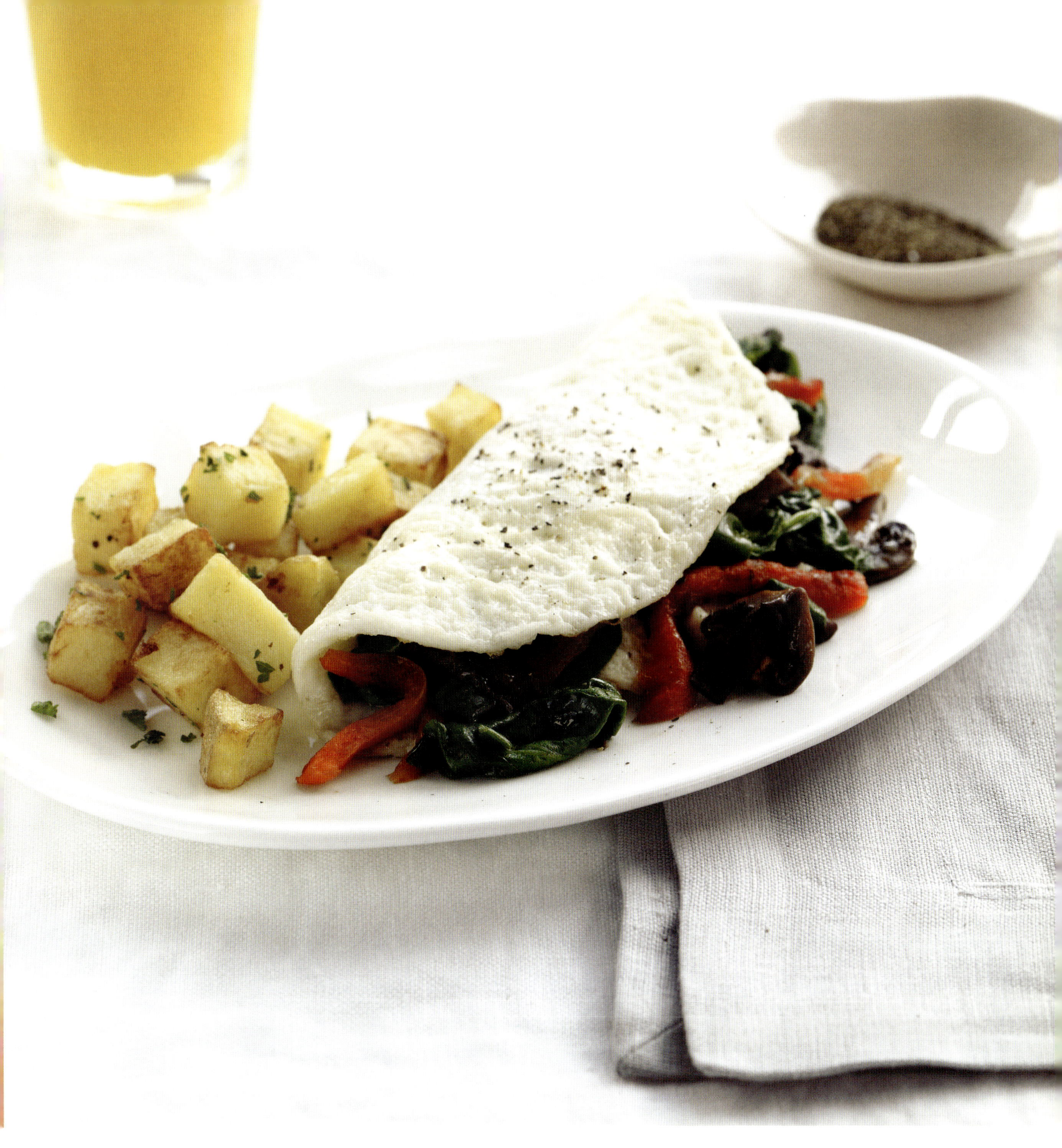

tofu scramble

Serves 4

Crumbled tofu mimics the texture of scrambled eggs, and shiitake mushrooms and tamari add an Asian twist to this savory breakfast. An unexpected flavor boost comes from tahini, a thick sesame seed paste. Look for jars of tahini in Middle Eastern markets, natural foods stores, and many well-stocked supermarkets.

Heat a 10-inch skillet over medium heat. Add the oil, tilting the pan to coat. When the oil is hot, add the mushrooms. Cook, stirring occasionally, until the mushrooms are softened but not browned, about 3 minutes.

Stir in the tofu, green onions, tahini, and curry powder. Cook for 2 minutes to blend the flavors. Stir in the tamari sauce and remove from the heat. If desired, garnish each serving with 1 tablespoon of sprouts.

78 cal, 13 g fat, 11 g prot, 7 g carb

1	teaspoon sesame or olive oil
4	ounces fresh shiitake mushrooms, stemmed and sliced (about 1 cup)
2	cups (about 12 ounces) crumbled firm tofu
2	green onions (scallions), chopped
¼	cup tahini (sesame seed paste)
1	teaspoon curry powder
2	tablespoons tamari sauce
4	tablespoons alfalfa, onion, or other sprouts, for garnish

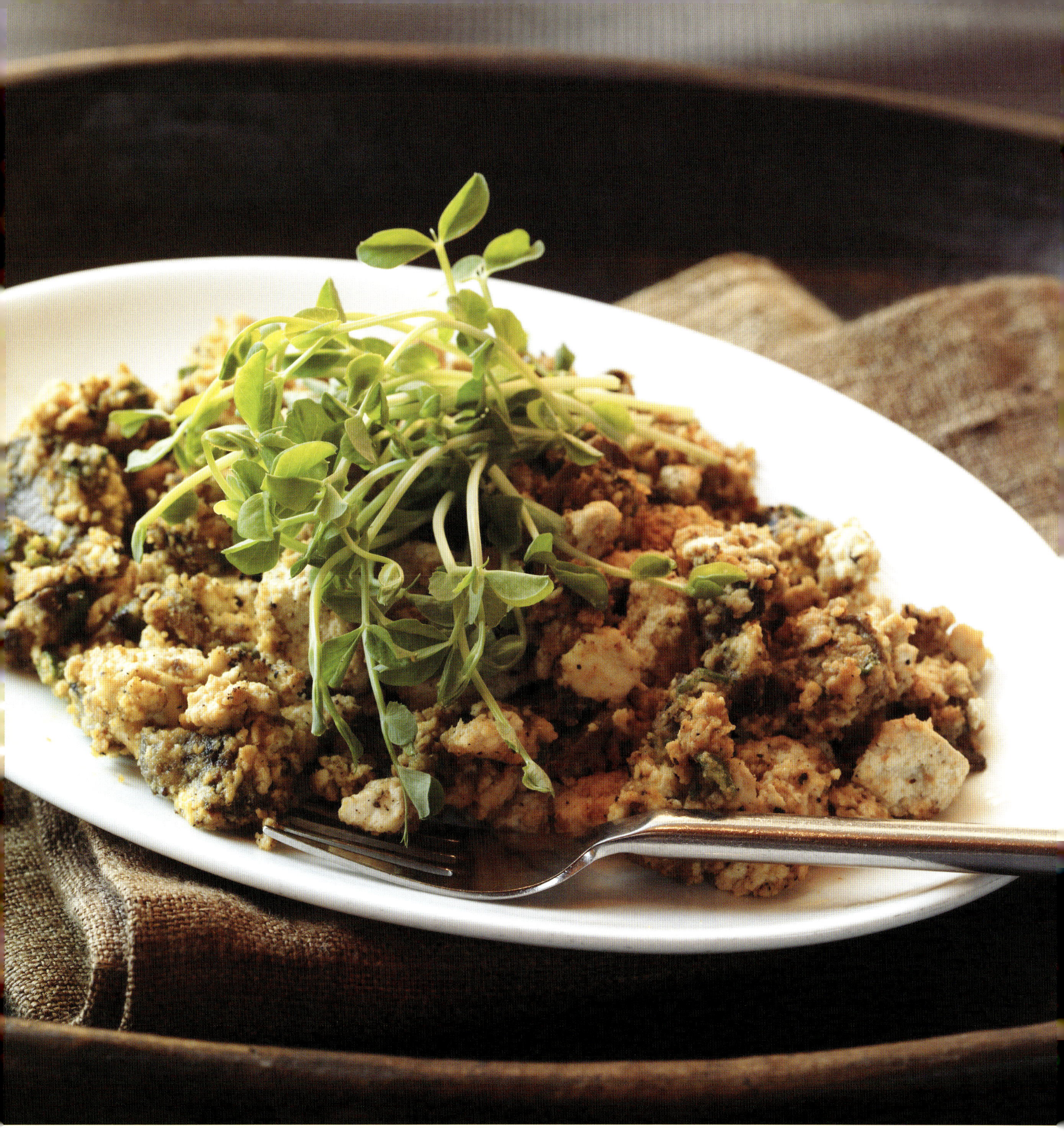

cinnamon french toast

Makes 8 to 10 slices, to serve 4 to 5

We use our own house-made cinnamon bread to make French toast for guests at Mii amo, but you can use any bread you have on hand. This is also a good way to use up stale slices or other forgotten bits of bread you may have stashed in the freezer. Serve this fragrant favorite with fresh berries, a dusting of powdered sugar, or an extra drizzle of pure maple syrup.

In a 9-inch pie plate or other shallow dish, combine the milk, egg whites, sugar, maple syrup, cinnamon, and vanilla. Whisk to blend well.

Spray a griddle or large skillet with nonstick cooking spray and preheat until hot. Dip a slice of bread into the egg white mixture, pressing down gently to saturate both sides. Transfer it to the griddle and cook, turning once, until nicely browned on both sides, about 4 minutes total. Keep warm. Repeat with the remaining bread slices. To serve, cut the bread slices in half and divide equally among warm plates. Top with berries, powdered sugar, or a light drizzle of maple syrup and serve at once.

302 cal, 1 g fat, 17 g prot, 59 g carb

1	cup nonfat milk
3	large egg whites
2	tablespoons sugar
1	tablespoon pure maple syrup
1¼	teaspoons ground cinnamon
¾	teaspoon vanilla extract

8 to 10 slices bread, ½ inch thick

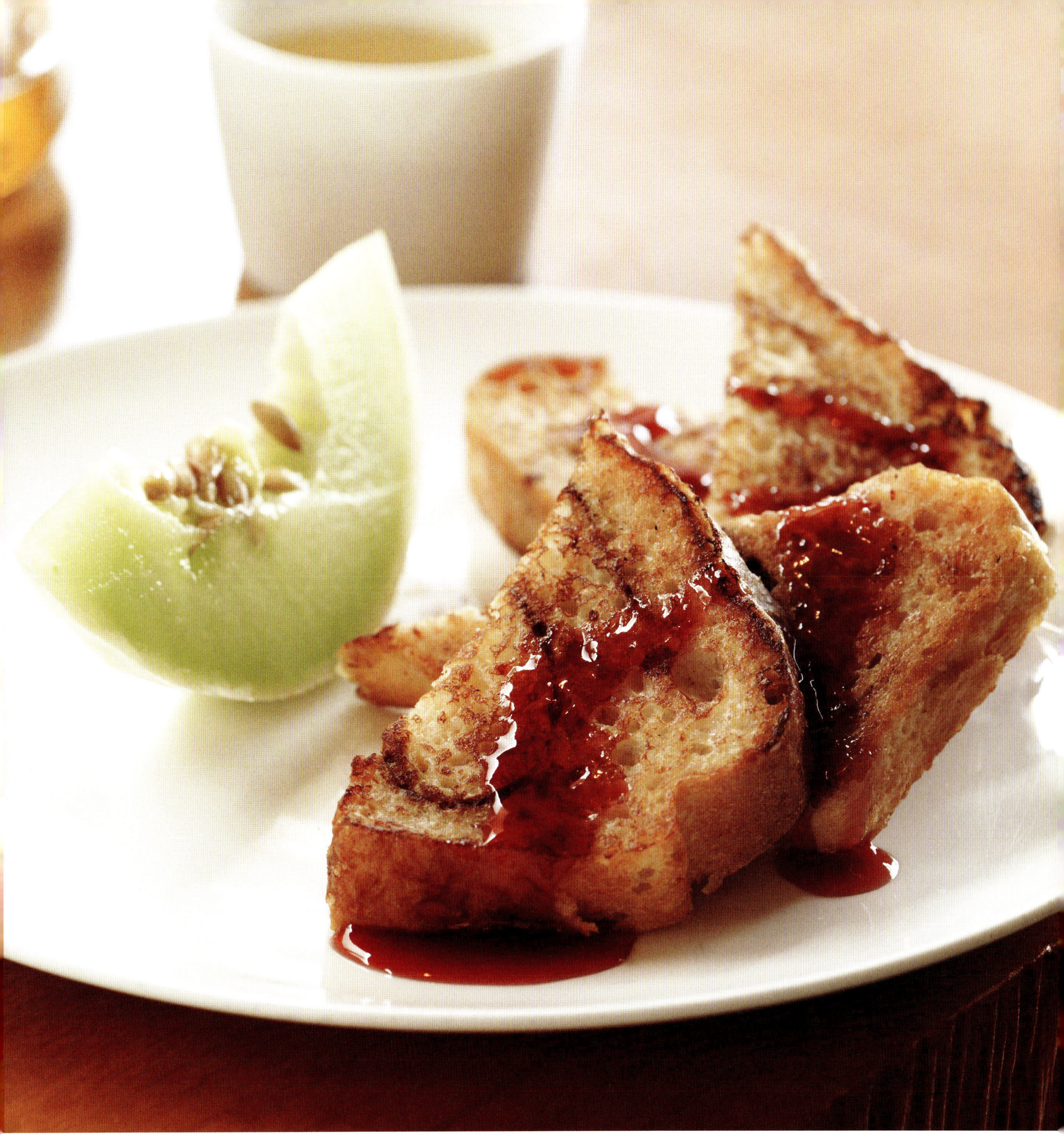

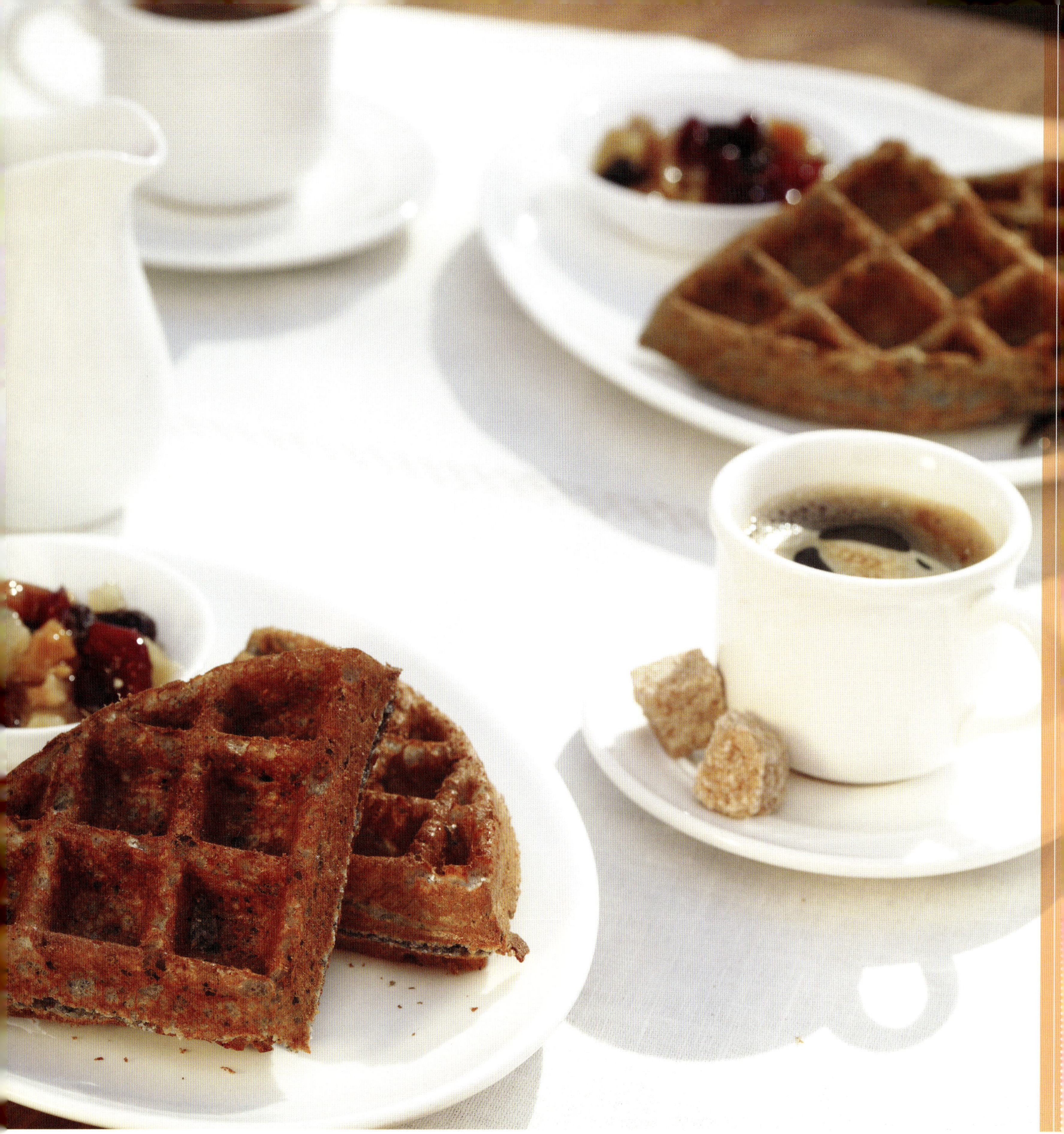

blue corn waffles
with dried fruit compote /p. 49

Makes eight 4-inch square waffles, to serve 8

With a supply of homemade waffle mix in the pantry, this batter comes together in minutes—making it ideal for weekday breakfasts. Although yellow cornmeal is an acceptable substitute, for authentic southwestern flavor look for blue cornmeal in natural foods stores and specialty markets.

Spray a waffle iron with nonstick cooking spray and preheat according to the manufacturer's directions. In a large bowl, whisk together the buttermilk and egg until well blended. Fold in the waffle mix until evenly moistened.

Pour about 1 cup of the batter into the waffle iron and cook as recommended by the manufacturer, until cooked through and nicely browned on the outside. Keep the waffles warm while you cook the remaining batter. Serve with 1 tablespoon of the compote, if desired.

82 cal, 2 g fat, 4 g prot, 13 g carb

1 cup Blue Corn Waffle Mix (recipe follows)
1 ⅛ cups low-fat buttermilk
1 large egg

Dried Fruit Compote (recipe follows; optional)

blue corn waffle mix

Makes about 4 cups

In a large bowl, combine the cornmeal, flour, baking powder, baking soda, salt, and sugar. Whisk gently to blend well. Use at once, or store in an airtight container in the refrigerator. The waffle mix should be kept cold, as warmth encourages the gluten and turns the mix lumpy.

- 2 cups blue cornmeal
- 2 cups all-purpose flour
- 2 tablespoons baking powder
- 2 teaspoons baking soda
- 2 teaspoons coarse (kosher) salt
- ¾ teaspoon brown sugar

dried fruit compote

Makes 1 cup

Simmer the fruit and juice together until almost dry. Serve warm or cool and refrigerate until needed, up to one week.

37 cal, 0.5 g fat, 0.5 g prot, 9 g carb

1	cup diced dried fruit mix
1	cup apple juice

carrot-bran muffins

Serves 12

In this recipe, a generous dose of spices transforms a humble vegetable into a sweet and fragrant muffin. Serve however many are needed for breakfast guests, and freeze the rest to enjoy throughout the week.

Preheat the oven to 325°F. Spray a 12-cup muffin tin with nonstick cooking spray or line it with paper liners. In a medium bowl, combine the flour, bran, baking powder, baking soda, cinnamon, ginger, and nutmeg. Whisk gently to blend.

In a large bowl, whisk together the buttermilk, honey, and egg whites until well blended. Add the dry ingredients, folding until nearly blended. Fold in the carrot. Divide the batter evenly among the muffin cups, filling each about two-thirds full. Bake until the muffins spring back when touched gently on top and a toothpick inserted into the center comes out clean, about 30 minutes. Transfer the muffins to a wire rack to cool. Serve slightly warm or at room temperature.

112 cal, 1 g fat, 5 g prot, 25 g carb

1¼	cups whole wheat flour
1	cup wheat bran
2	teaspoons baking powder
¾	teaspoon baking soda
¾	teaspoon ground cinnamon
½	teaspoon ground ginger
¼	teaspoon freshly grated nutmeg
1	cup low-fat buttermilk
½	cup honey
4	large egg whites
1	carrot, coarsely grated (about 1 cup)

cranberry-orange bread

Makes one 9 x 5 x 3–inch loaf, to serve about 16

Crimson cranberries punctuate this fragrant whole-grain loaf, making a special addition to the breakfast table. Baked loaves freeze perfectly when wrapped airtight, so double the recipe if you like.

Preheat the oven to 350°F. Coat a 9 x 5 x 3–inch loaf pan with nonstick cooking spray. In a medium bowl, combine the flour, bran, sugar, dry milk, baking powder, and cinnamon. Whisk gently to blend.

In a large bowl, whisk together the buttermilk, honey, and egg whites until well blended. Add the dry ingredients, folding until nearly blended. Fold in the cranberries and orange zest.

Scrape the batter into the prepared pan and bake until the center springs back when touched gently on top and a toothpick inserted into the center comes out clean, about 50 minutes. Let cool in the pan for 10 minutes, then invert onto a wire rack to cool completely. Cut into slices to serve.

59 cal, 1 g fat, 2 g prot, 13 g carb

1⅓ cups whole wheat flour
⅔ cup wheat bran
½ cup sugar
1 tablespoon nonfat dry milk powder
2 teaspoons baking powder
½ teaspoon ground cinnamon
1 cup low-fat buttermilk
¼ cup honey
3 large egg whites
1½ cups fresh or frozen cranberries, coarsely chopped

Finely grated zest of 1 orange

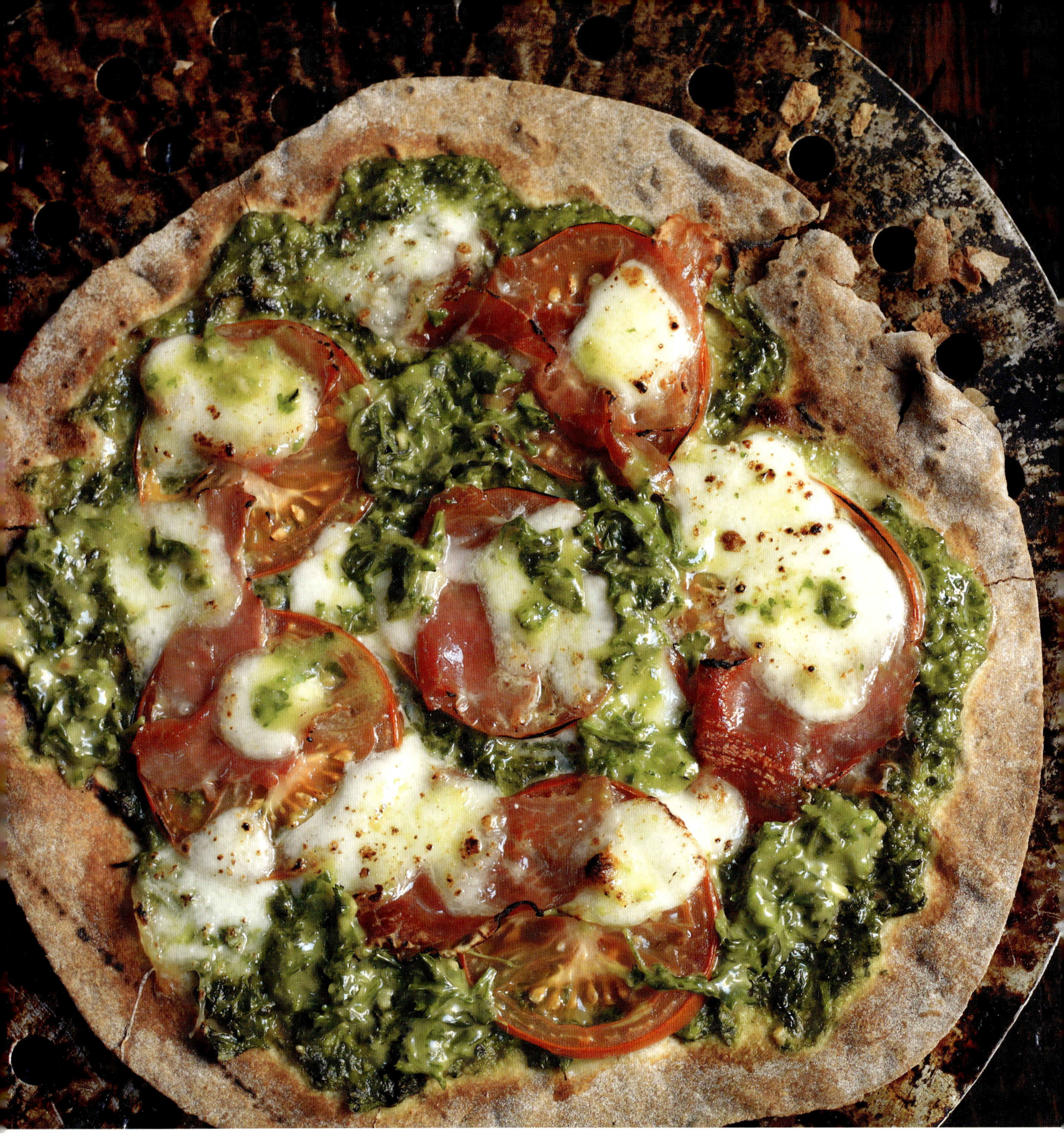

Lunch

tomato gazpacho

Makes about 6 ¾ cups, to serve 6

Think of this refreshing soup as liquid salsa—plenty of garden-fresh flavors in a bowl. Depending upon the acid content of the tomatoes, you may need to add an extra teaspoon or two of vinegar at the end to perk up the taste. If craving gazpacho in the winter when no good tomatoes are available, substitute the best-quality canned tomatoes you can find. This tastes best when allowed to marinate overnight.

Working in batches as needed, combine the tomatoes, cucumber, onion, bell pepper, cilantro, basil, both vinegars, oregano, garlic, and oil in a blender or food processor. Process, pulsing the machine on and off, until the vegetables are finely chopped and have released their juices. Pour the mixture into a large bowl and season to taste with salt and pepper. If needed, add more white balsamic vinegar to balance the flavors. Cover and refrigerate for at least 2 hours or overnight to blend flavors. Serve chilled.

82 cal, 2 g fat, 4 g prot, 16 g carb

7	cups coarsely chopped tomatoes (about 10 medium tomatoes, seeded)
2	cups coarsely chopped English (hothouse) cucumber, peeled
1	cup coarsely chopped red onion
1	cup coarsely chopped red bell pepper
1	bunch fresh cilantro, coarsely chopped (about 2 cups)
6	fresh basil leaves, torn in half
2	tablespoons red wine vinegar
2	tablespoons white balsamic vinegar, or as needed
1	tablespoon fresh oregano
1	teaspoon minced garlic
1	teaspoon extra-virgin olive oil

Salt
Freshly ground pepper

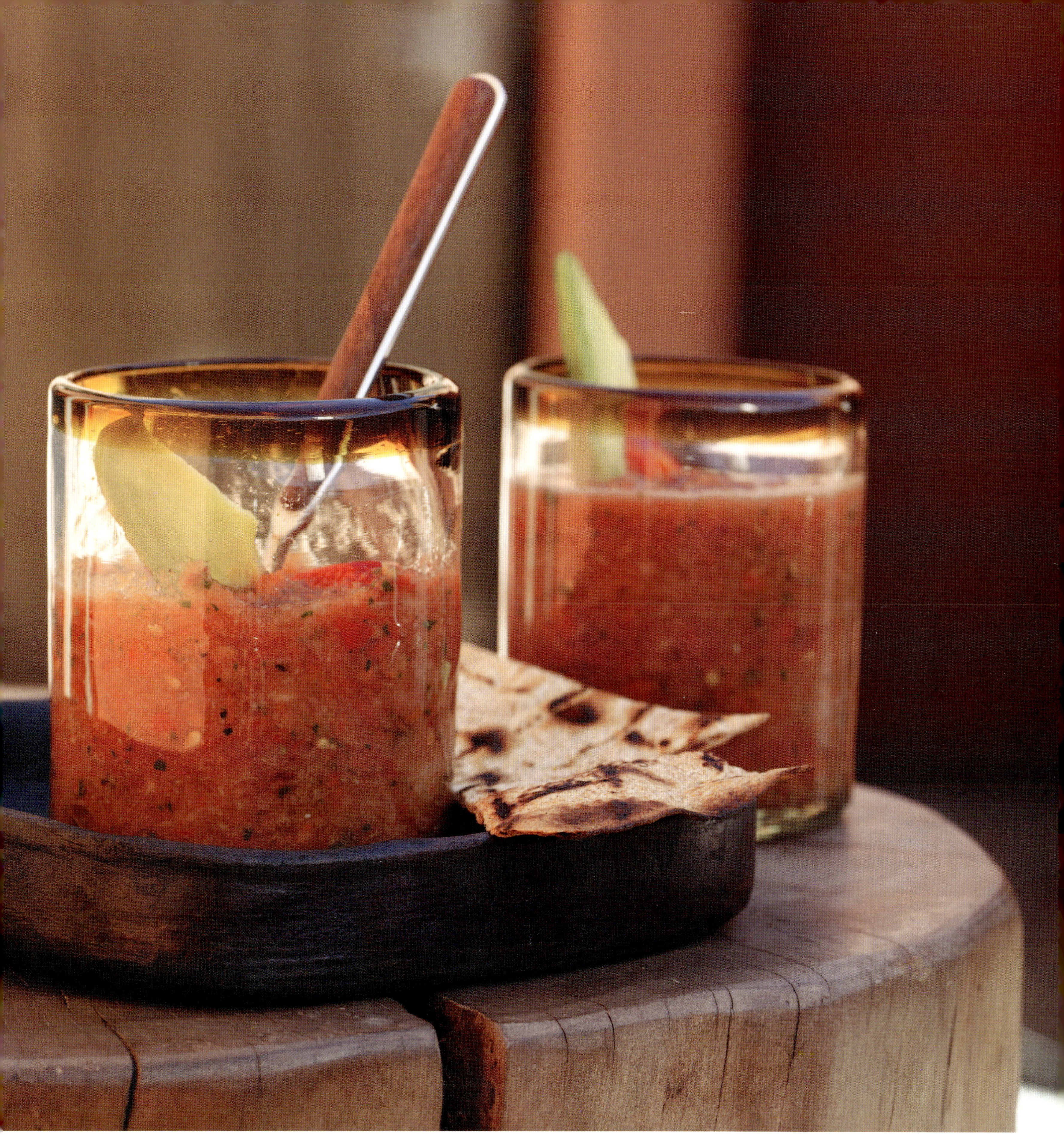

asian chicken salad
with miso-mango vinaigrette /p. 57

Serves 4

Asian-style chicken salads are a perennial lunch favorite. Instead of relying on an overly salty-sweet dressing, ours gets its flavor from crisp fresh vegetables and a gingery mango vinaigrette made with vitamin-rich miso, a Japanese fermented soybean paste. Although the following recipe gives instructions for cooking chicken breasts, this salad is a delicious way to use leftover roast chicken.

Rinse the chicken with cold water and pat dry with paper towels. Season with salt and pepper. Spray a grill pan or skillet with nonstick cooking spray and place it over medium-high heat until hot. Add the chicken breasts and cook, turning once or twice, until opaque throughout but still juicy, about 10 minutes total. Set aside to cool, then cut diagonally into thin slices.

Bring a medium pot of salted water to a boil. Add the snow peas and carrot. As soon as the water returns to a boil, drain the vegetables in a colander and refresh them under cold running water to stop the cooking. Drain well.

In a large bowl, combine the chicken, snow peas, carrot, cabbage, bok choy, mango, and cucumber. Drizzle with the vinaigrette and toss gently to mix.

Heat the rice paper on a hot grill just until crisp. Break into large pieces. Divide the salad among 4 large plates and sprinkle with the sesame seeds. Stand 1 or 2 pieces of crisp rice paper in the center of each salad and serve at once.

286 cal, 5 g fat, 38 g prot, 20 g carb

- ¾ cup Miso-Mango Vinaigrette (recipe follows)
- 1 pound skinless boneless chicken breast halves or 2 cups shredded cooked chicken
- 8 ounces snow peas, trimmed, halved if large
- 1 large carrot, cut into matchstick-sized pieces
- 2 cups thinly sliced napa cabbage
- 2 cups thinly sliced bok choy
- 1 cup finely diced mango
- ½ cup finely diced seeded cucumber
- 2 sheets edible Japanese rice paper, for garnish (optional)
- 1 tablespoon toasted white sesame seeds, for garnish

Salt
Freshly ground pepper

miso-mango vinaigrette

Makes about 1 cup

In a small saucepan, boil the orange juice over medium-high heat until reduced by half, about 10 minutes. Let cool.

In a blender or food processor, combine the orange juice, mango, vinegar, miso, ginger, and garlic. Process until smooth. With the machine running, add the stock, flax seed oil, and sesame oil until well blended. Use at once, or refrigerate for up to 24 hours.

Note: Miso is available in Japanese markets, natural foods stores, and in the Asian foods section of many well-stocked supermarkets.

2	tablespoons Thickened Vegetable Stock (page 79)
1	cup fresh orange juice
½	cup chopped mango
2	tablespoons rice vinegar
1	tablespoon white miso paste (see Note)
1	teaspoon finely grated fresh ginger
1	clove garlic, minced
1	tablespoons flax seed oil
½	teaspoon Asian sesame oil

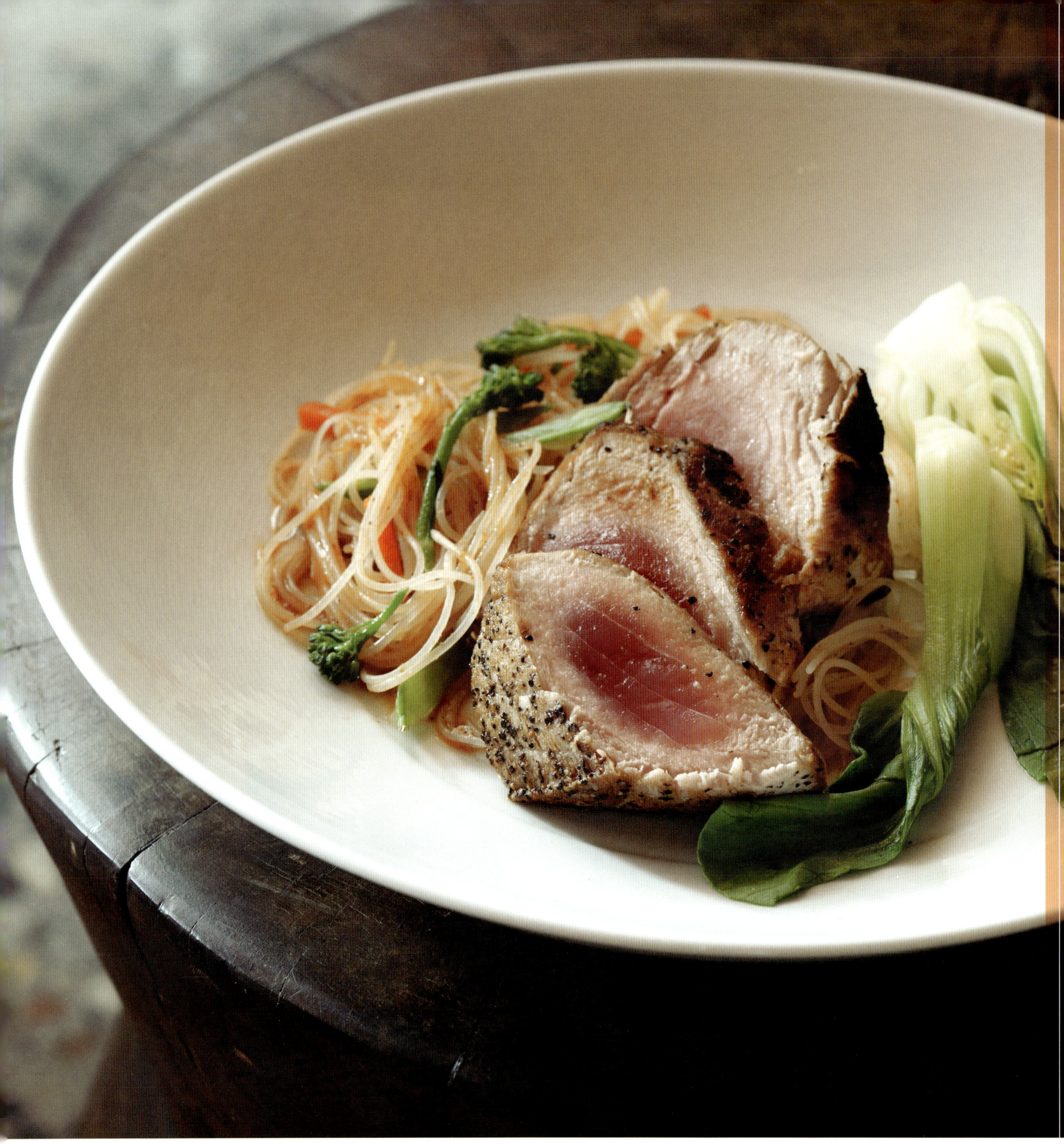

pan-seared ahi tuna with cellophane noodles and red curry broth /p. 60

Serves 4

Unfortunately, there are no bargains in the world of seafood. At Mii amo, we routinely use the finest quality sashimi-grade tuna, and we think our dishes speak for themselves. Seek out a reputable fishmonger in your area so you, too, can get the most for your money. For a presentation that is as colorful as it is healthy and delicious, the noodles are tossed with steamed vegetables such as snow peas, broccolini, baby carrots, and bok choy.

Put the noodles in a large bowl and add enough warm water to cover. Let stand until soft, about 10 minutes. Drain well and toss with the sesame oil and sesame seeds.

Heat a cast-iron skillet or other heavy pan over high heat until hot. Rub the tuna steaks all over with the olive oil and season with salt and pepper. Cook, turning once, until nicely browned on the outside and cooked to the desired doneness inside, 6 to 8 minutes total for medium-rare. Let the steaks rest in a warm spot for 3 to 5 minutes.

Toss the noodles with the steamed vegetables. Mound one fourth of the noodle mixture in the center of each of 4 warmed, large, shallow soup bowls or plates, forming a nest. Slice each tuna steak into 3 diagonal slices and place them on top of the noodles. Drizzle each serving with about 3 tablespoons of Red Curry Broth and serve at once.

Note: Any type of rice noodle will work for this recipe. There are a couple of different ways to cook them. The bean thread noodles cook quickly. Soak them in hot water for 10 minutes, then toss them with vegetables and sauce. You can even dip them in hot water to reheat them. If using a thicker rice noodle, they should be soaked in cold water for 10 to 15 minutes, then cooked in boiling water. They can be reheated in hot water or tossed with sauce and vegetables.

374 cal, 10 g fat, 28 g prot, 40 g carb

- ¾ cup Red Curry Broth (recipe follows)
- 4 ounces dried cellophane (bean thread) noodles (see Note)
- 1 tablespoon Asian sesame oil
- 1½ teaspoons toasted sesame seeds
- 4 tuna steaks, cut 1 inch thick, each weighing about 4 ounces
- 1 teaspoon olive oil

Salt

Freshly ground pepper

About 4 cups assorted steamed seasonal vegetables

red curry broth

Makes about ¾ cup

In a medium skillet, bring the stock to a boil over high heat. Boil until thickened and reduced to about one third of its original volume, 5 to 7 minutes. Reduce the heat to medium-low and whisk in the curry paste, tamari, mirin, and sugar. Cook, whisking occasionally, until the flavors have blended, about 10 minutes.

Note: Prepared Thai curry pastes are available at Asian grocery stores and in the Asian foods section of many supermarkets. They are spicy products, so use according to taste.

2	cups Vegetable Stock (page 63)
1	tablespoon prepared Thai red curry paste (see Note)
1	tablespoon tamari
1	tablespoon mirin (Japanese rice wine)
1½	teaspoons sugar

salmon and spinach risotto
with red wine glaze /p. 62

Serves 4

Our chefs don't feel that risotto needs to be swimming in fat to taste good. Instead, they use the highest quality ingredients and let the natural flavors shine through. For this recipe, the risotto and fish are supplemented with a side of fresh vegetables, such as asparagus and baby carrots.

Put the spinach in a medium saucepan and season with salt and pepper. Cover and cook over low heat until wilted, about 1 minute. Stir in about 1 cup of the warm stock and remove from the heat. Using a handheld immersion blender, puree the mixture until smooth. (Alternatively, let cool slightly and puree in a food processor or blender.) Stir the spinach mixture into the remaining stock. Do not wash the saucepan.

In the same saucepan, heat the oil over medium heat until hot. Stir in the rice and cook to brown a bit. Add the onion and garlic, stirring, until the grains appear translucent around the edges, 1 to 2 minutes. Add about ½ cup of the hot stock-spinach mixture and cook, stirring, until the rice has absorbed the liquid, about 2 minutes. Adjust the heat as needed to maintain a simmer. Continue stirring constantly, adding the hot stock mixture about ½ cup at a time and letting it absorb fully before adding more, until the rice is creamy and tender yet still firm to the bite, 20 to 25 minutes total. Stir in the cheese. Season with salt and pepper to taste. Keep warm.

Season both sides of the salmon fillets with salt and pepper and sprinkle with the herbs, pressing down gently to make them adhere. Spray a medium skillet, preferably nonstick, with nonstick cooking spray. Warm over medium heat until hot. Working in batches if needed, cook the salmon, turning once, until nicely browned on the outside and just barely pink throughout, 4 to 6 minutes total.

Mound one fourth of the risotto in the center of each of 4 warmed dinner plates. Place a salmon fillet on top of each and drizzle with 1 tablespoon of Red Wine Glaze. Serve at once.

378 cal, 9 g fat, 27 g prot, 47 g carb

¼	cup Red Wine Glaze (recipe follows)
3	cups Vegetable Stock (recipe follows), heated
4	cups (about 4 ounces) baby spinach leaves, rinsed but not dried
1	teaspoon olive oil
1	cup Arborio rice
2	tablespoons finely diced yellow onion
1	teaspoon minced garlic
4	teaspoons freshly grated Parmesan cheese, preferably Parmigiano-Reggiano
4	skinless, boneless salmon fillets, about 4 ounces each
1	teaspoon herbes de Provence or other dried herb seasoning blend

Salt
Freshly ground pepper

red wine glaze

Makes ¼ cup

In a small skillet or saucepan, heat the wine over high heat until reduced by half. Add the corn syrup, continuing to cook until it reaches a syrupy consistency, 2 to 3 minutes more.

1 cup dry red wine

2 tablespoons light corn syrup

vegetable stock

Makes about 8 cups

The secret to many of our great soups and sauces is an intensely flavored homemade stock. This fat-free version is simmered slowly to draw maximum flavor from all of the ingredients.

In a stockpot, combine the onions, tomatoes, celery, carrots, mushrooms, leeks, fennel, garlic, peppercorns, parsley, thyme, and oregano. Pour in the water. Bring to a boil over high heat, then reduce the heat to low and simmer for 1 hour.

Strain the stock through a sieve and discard the solids. Use at once, or cool and refrigerate for up to 4 days. Freeze for longer storage.

- 3 cups chopped yellow onions
- 2 tomatoes, quartered and seeded
- 1 cup chopped celery
- 1 cup chopped carrots
- 1 cup chopped mushrooms
- ½ cup chopped leeks (white and tender green leaves)
- ½ cup coarsely chopped fennel bulb (optional)
- 4 cloves garlic, halved
- 1 tablespoon whole black peppercorns
- 1½ teaspoons dried parsley
- 1½ teaspoons dried thyme
- 1½ teaspoons dried oregano
- 8 cups cold water

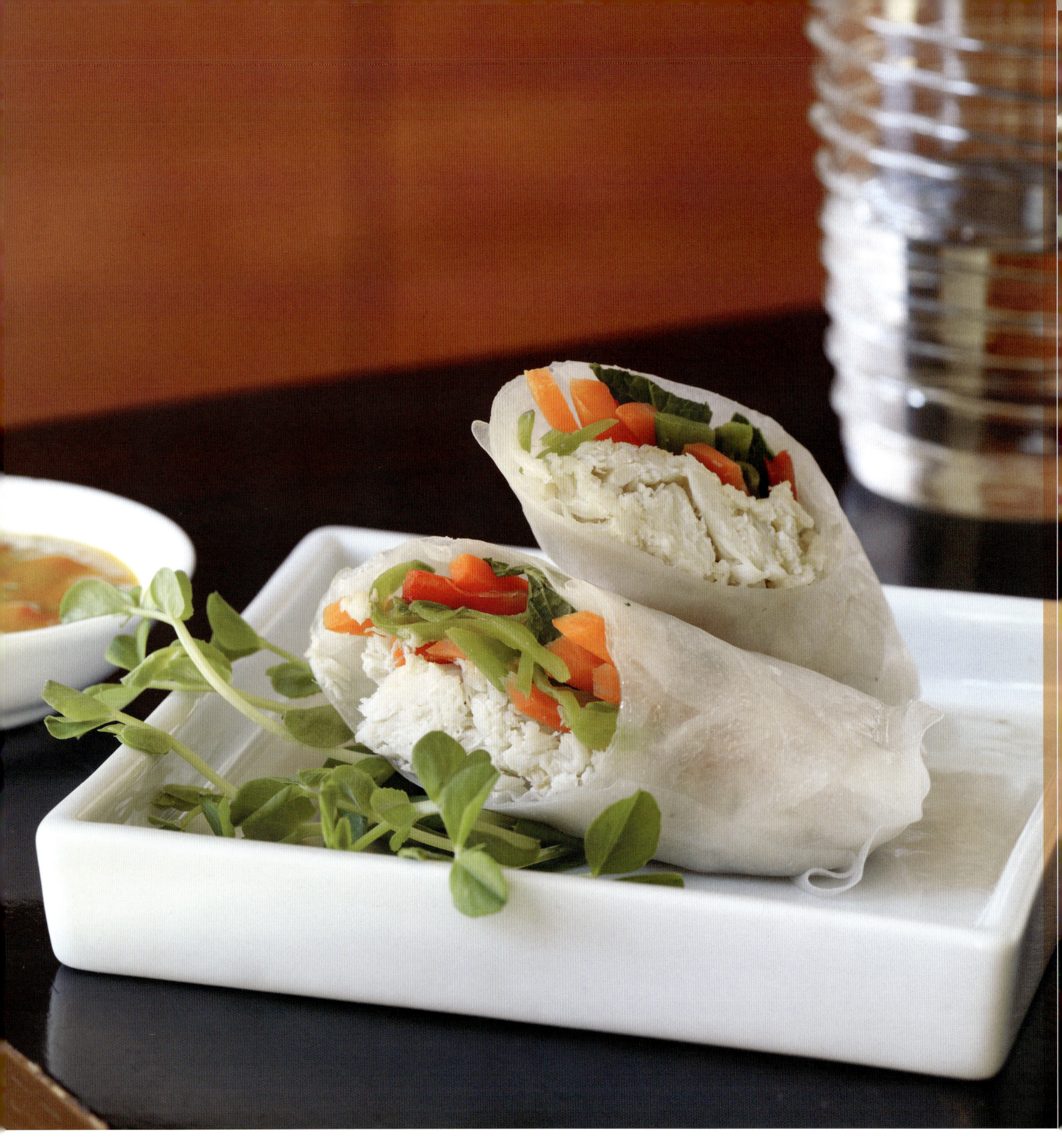

crab spring rolls
with mango-chile dipping sauce /p. 66

Makes 4 spring rolls, to serve 4

Spicy, sweet, crunchy, and cool—this light entrée embodies all the refreshing flavors and textures that make Southeast Asian foods so popular. Edible rice paper is usually sold in cellophane packages containing eight or more pieces. Look for them in Asian grocery stores and in the Asian foods section of many supermarkets. The papers last indefinitely when stored airtight at room temperature.

In a small skillet, heat the sesame oil over medium heat until hot but not smoking. Add the snow peas, red bell pepper, and 1½ tablespoons of the carrot. Cook, stirring and tossing, until crisp-tender, 1 to 2 minutes. Scrape the mixture into a large bowl and set aside to cool.

Add the crab to the cooled vegetable mixture, tossing gently to mix.

In a shallow bowl, working with 1 at a time, soak the rice paper in hot tap water just until soft and pliable, about 45 seconds. Carefully remove it from the water, shaking off any excess, and lay it on a flat work surface. Spoon one fourth of the crab mixture down the center and sprinkle with 1 teaspoon of the mint. Fold in the top and bottom edges of the paper to enclose the filling, then roll to form a tight cylinder. Place it seam-side down. Repeat with remaining rice paper and filling. (The rolls can be kept at cool room temperature for up to 1 hour when covered with a damp paper towel. If longer, refrigerate.)

Cut each spring roll in half diagonally and arrange it on a plate. Top each roll with 1 tablespoon each of sprouts and additional carrot. Drizzle the chile sauce over the plate for garnish. Serve at once with ¼ cup of the dipping sauce on the side.

Note: Sriracha hot chile sauce is available at Asian grocery stores and in the Asian foods section of many supermarkets.

160 cal, 3 g fat, 13 g prot, 21 g carb

- 1 cup Mango-Chile Dipping Sauce (recipe follows)
- 2 teaspoons Asian sesame oil
- 1½ tablespoons matchstick-sized pieces snow peas
- 1½ tablespoons matchstick-sized pieces red bell pepper
- ⅓ cup matchstick-sized pieces carrot, divided
- 8 ounces crabmeat, drained and picked over to remove shells and cartilage
- 4 pieces edible dried rice paper (spring roll skins), each about 8½ inches
- 4 teaspoons minced fresh mint
- 4 tablespoons daikon sprouts
- 4 teaspoons Sriracha hot chile sauce (see Note)

mango-chile dipping sauce

Makes about 1 cup

Blend all ingredients together.

1	cup mango puree
2	tablespoons rice vinegar
1	tablespoon tamari sauce
1	tablespoon minced green onion (scallion)
1	tablespoon fresh cilantro, chopped
½	teaspoon minced fresh ginger
½	teaspoon minced garlic
½	teaspoon Sriracha hot chile sauce

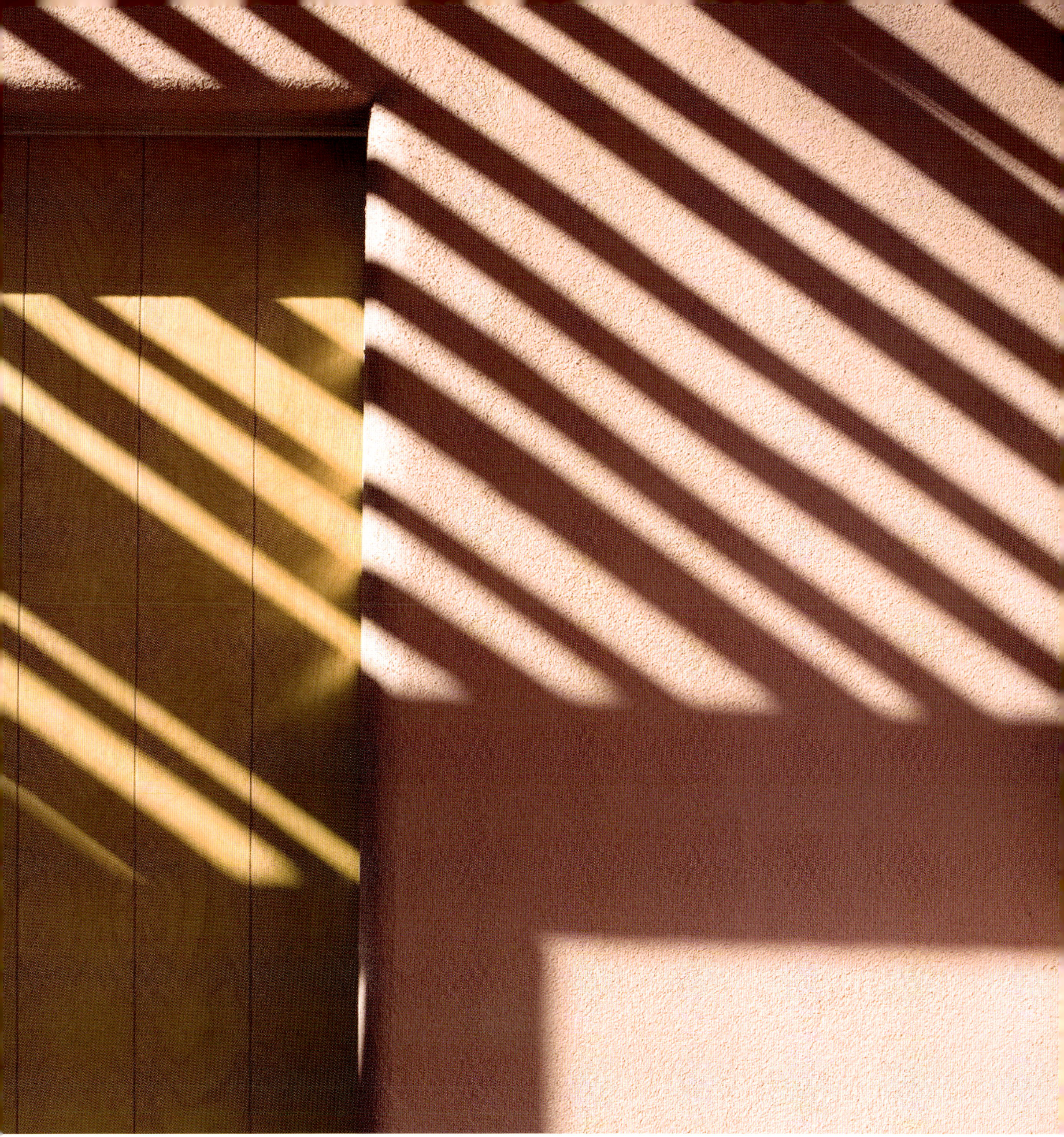

vegetarian chili

Makes about 4 cups, to serve 4 to 6

Don't be alarmed by the number of ingredients—once everything is added to the pot, this zesty chili requires little attention until serving time. For a delicious presentation, the finished chili can be ladled over an edible "bowl" of acorn squash and garnished with classic chili fixings. If you like your chili extra-spicy, add a bit of minced jalapeño along with the poblano chile pepper.

Prepare the Vegetable Stock ahead of time. Warm the oil in a large saucepan over medium heat. Add the eggplant, corn, onion, celery, and carrot and cook, stirring occasionally, until softened but not browned, about 5 minutes. Stir in the bell pepper, poblano, and garlic and cook 3 minutes longer. Stir in the tomato paste, cilantro, thyme, and oregano and cook for 2 minutes, then stir in the stock, tomatoes, black beans, garbanzo beans, salt, paprika, chile powder, cumin, coriander, and pepper. Cook uncovered, stirring occasionally and adjusting the heat as needed to avoid the mixture from boiling vigorously, until the flavors have blended and the chili is thick, about 45 minutes. If the chili is too thick, stir in a bit more stock or water.

To serve, sprinkle evenly with the cheese and green onions, and top each serving with a small dollop of sour cream. Serve at once.

Another serving option: In a large pot fitted with a steamer basket, bring about 2 inches of water to a boil over high heat. Cut 2 small acorn squash in half lengthwise. Scoop out and discard the seeds and fibers. Using tongs or a large spoon, place the squash halves on the steamer basket, cut-sides down. Cover the pot and reduce the heat to medium-low. Cook until the squash is tender when pierced with the tip of a sharp knife, 15 to 20 minutes.

To serve, place 1 squash half, cut-side up, in each of 4 shallow bowls. (If needed, cut a thin slice from the bottom of each squash half so it will lie flat.) Ladle chili into the cavity of each squash, letting some of it overflow into the bowl. Garnish as above. Serve at once.

264 cal, 2 g fat, 10 g prot, 12 g carb

2½	cups Vegetable Stock (page 63), or as needed
2	teaspoons olive oil
1	small eggplant, chopped
¾	cup fresh or frozen corn kernels
1	small onion, chopped
1	small rib celery, chopped
1	small carrot, chopped
⅓	cup chopped green bell pepper
3	tablespoons chopped poblano chile pepper
2	teaspoons minced garlic
2	teaspoons tomato paste
1½	tablespoons chopped fresh cilantro
½	teaspoon dried thyme
½	teaspoon dried oregano
1	cup drained canned diced tomatoes
¾	cup cooked or canned black beans, drained
¾	cup cooked or canned garbanzo beans, drained
½	teaspoon salt
½	teaspoon paprika
½	teaspoon chile powder
¼	teaspoon ground cumin
¼	teaspoon ground coriander
¼	teaspoon ground white pepper
4	tablespoons reduced-fat shredded Cheddar or Monterey Jack cheese
2	tablespoons chopped green onion (scallion)
4	teaspoons low-fat or nonfat sour cream
2	small acorn squash (optional)

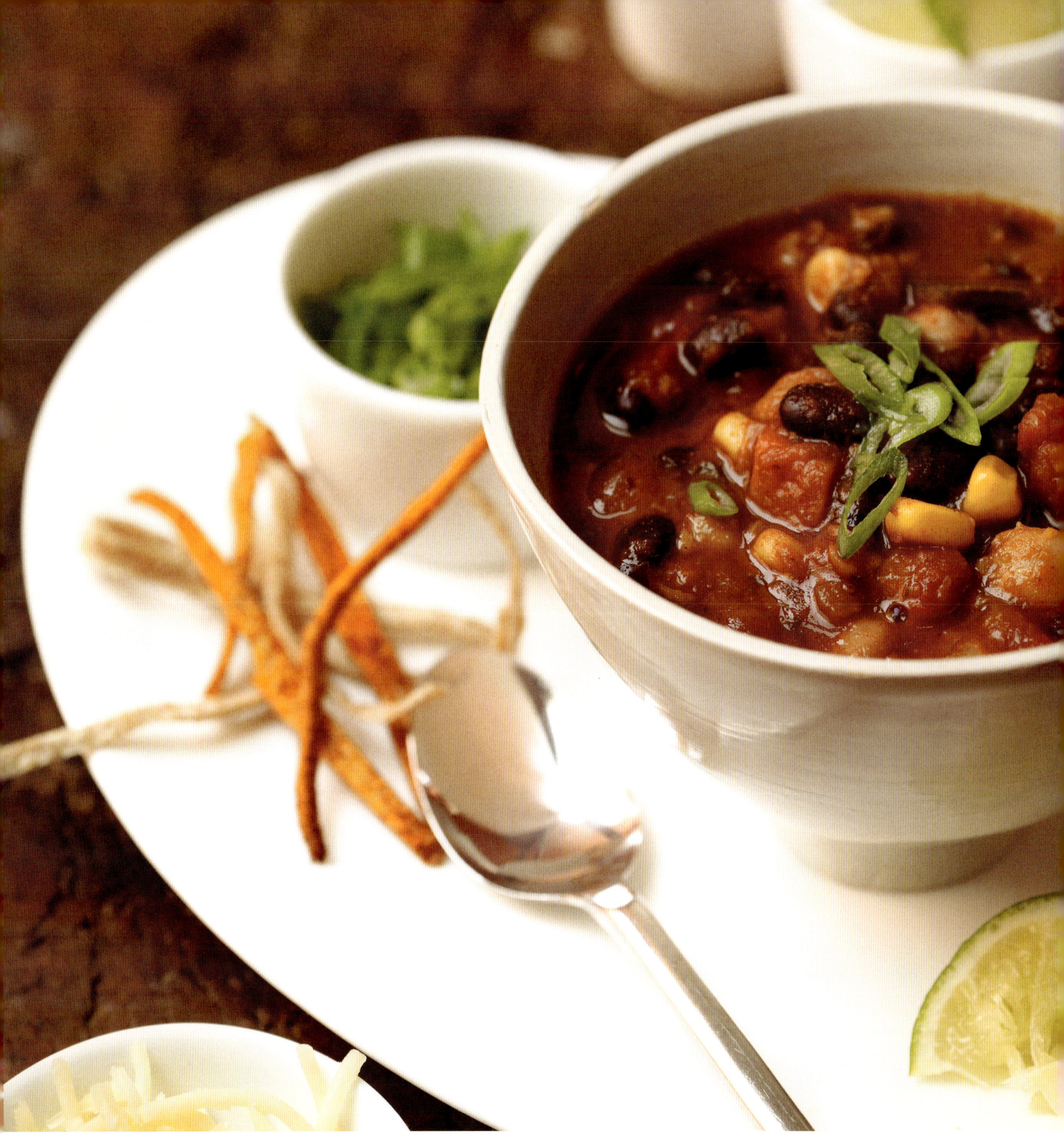

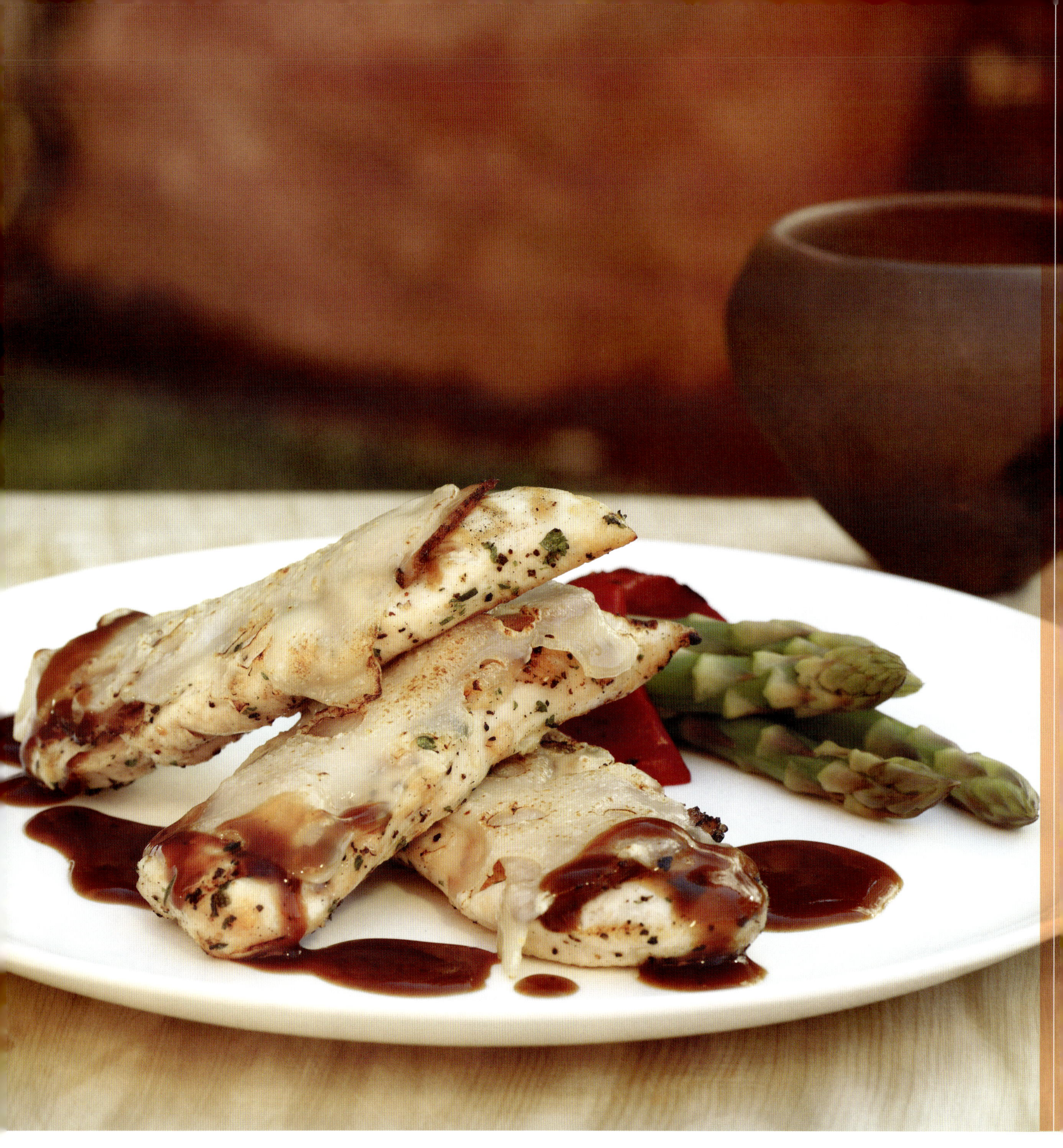

chicken napoleon
with cabernet jus /p. 72

Serves 4

Although this napoleon is almost as beautiful as its sweet namesake, it packs a lot more flavor and considerably fewer calories. Tasso is spicy cured and smoked pork shoulder often used in Cajun cuisine. Look for it in specialty food markets; just a few slices transform ordinary chicken into a rich treat.

Preheat a stovetop grill pan or cast-iron skillet until hot. Rinse the chicken with cold water and pat dry with paper towels. Place 1 chicken tender between 2 sheets of plastic wrap and pound with the bottom of a heavy pot to an even thickness of ⅛ to ⅜ inch. Repeat with the remaining tenders, making all approximately the same size and shape. Season to taste with salt and pepper. Working in batches, grill the chicken tenders, turning once, until white throughout but still juicy, 2 to 3 minutes total.

On the same grill, working in batches if necessary, cook the tasso slices, turning once, until just heated through, about 1 minute. Top each chicken tender with a slice of tasso and a slice of cheese, letting it soften and melt slightly. Stack 3 tenders on each plate to form a napoleon. Keep warm.

In a large pot of boiling salted water, cook the asparagus until crisp-tender, 1 to 2 minutes, depending upon thickness. When just cool enough to handle, wrap 2 bell pepper strips around each spear to resemble a flower. Place 1 on each plate, resting it against the chicken napoleon. Drizzle 2 tablespoons of Cabernet Jus over each plate and serve at once.

262 cal, 7 g fat, 40 g prot, 6 g carb

- ½ cup Cabernet Jus (recipe follows), warm
- 18 ounces chicken tenders (about 12 tenders)
- 12 slices tasso ham, about ¼ ounce each
- 8 thin slices Gruyère cheese, about ½ ounce each, cut in half
- 4 large spears asparagus, trimmed
- 1 roasted red bell pepper, fresh or bottled, cut into 8 long strips

Salt
Freshly ground pepper

cabernet jus

Makes about 1 cup

Heat the oil in a medium skillet over medium heat. Add the mushrooms, shallot, garlic, thyme, peppercorns, and bay leaf. Cook, stirring occasionally, until the shallots are soft and the mushroom liquid has exuded and then evaporated, about 5 minutes.

Pour in the wine and increase the heat to high. Cook, stirring occasionally, for 5 to 7 minutes, or until the liquid has reduced to about ¼ cup. Add the veal stock and chicken stock and continue cooking over high heat until the liquid has thickened and reduced by half, 7 to 10 minutes. Strain the jus through a sieve and discard the solids. Season with salt and pepper to taste. Use at once, or refrigerate for up to 3 days; freeze for longer storage. Reheat gently before using.

1	teaspoon olive oil
½	cup chopped cremini mushrooms
¼	cup chopped shallot
½	teaspoon minced garlic
1	sprig fresh thyme
2	whole black peppercorns
1	small bay leaf
¾	cup Cabernet Sauvignon or other dry red wine
1	cup veal or chicken stock, purchased or homemade
1	cup (additional) chicken stock, purchased or homemade

Salt
Freshly ground pepper

veggie burger
with sweet onion ketchup /p. 74

Serves 6

We serve our veggie burgers with pita bread, crisp lettuce, vine-ripened tomato, pickle, and our own house-made Sweet Onion Ketchup.

In a food processor or blender, process the oats until finely ground. (You will have about 1 cup.) Set aside.

In a small heavy saucepan, combine the quinoa with ½ cup water. Bring to a boil over medium heat. Reduce the heat to low and cook, covered, until tender, 12 to 15 minutes.

Preheat the oven to 300°F. In a large bowl, combine the zucchini, squash, and carrots. Toss gently to mix. Spread the vegetables into an even layer on a rimmed baking sheet sprayed with nonstick cooking spray. Bake, stirring every 15 minutes, until the vegetables are lightly browned and any excess moisture has evaporated, 1 to 1½ hours. Let cool.

Spray a large sauté pan or skillet with nonstick cooking spray. Heat over medium heat until hot. Add the bell pepper, portabella mushrooms, cremini mushrooms, onion, and garlic. Season to taste with salt and pepper. Cook, stirring, until softened but not browned, 3 to 5 minutes. Stir in the parsley, thyme, and oregano and cook 1 minute longer. Let cool.

In a large bowl, combine the baked and cooled zucchini mixture with the sautéed and cooled vegetable mixture. Stir in the quinoa. Add 1 egg white, stirring to blend well. If needed, add more egg white until the vegetables are evenly coated. Stir in the ground oatmeal until well blended. Form the mixture into 6 patties, each about 4 inches round and ½ inch thick.

Spray a griddle or large skillet with nonstick cooking spray. Heat over medium heat until hot. Working in batches if necessary, cook the veggie burgers, turning once, until nicely browned on the outsides and cooked through, about 12 minutes total. Serve as noted above.

208 cal, 3 g fat, 13 g prot, 38 g carb

- 1½ cups Sweet Onion Ketchup (recipe follows)
- 1¼ cups old-fashioned rolled oats, such as Quaker Oats
- ¼ cup uncooked quinoa
- 1¾ cups (8 ounces) coarsely grated zucchini
- 1¾ cups (8 ounces) coarsely grated yellow squash
- 2 cups (8 ounces) coarsely grated carrots
- 1 red or green bell pepper, finely chopped
- 1½ cups (4 ounces) finely chopped portabella mushroom caps
- 1½ cups (4 ounces) finely chopped cremini mushrooms
- ¼ cup finely chopped red onion
- 1½ teaspoons minced garlic
- ¼ cup chopped fresh parsley
- ¾ teaspoon dried thyme
- ½ teaspoon dried oregano
- 1 to 3 large egg whites, as needed
- Salt
- Freshly ground pepper

sweet onion ketchup

Makes about 2 cups

Ketchup remains one of the most popular condiments in the country, so our chefs found a way to make it taste even better than the bottled stuff, and make it good for you, too. Slow-cooking the onions provides a deep, rich flavor you won't find anywhere in a bottle. If you can find a sweet yellow onion like a Vidalia or Maui, this will taste even better. If not, the caramelizing process below will bring out the onion's natural sweetness.

Spray a large sauté pan or Dutch oven with nonstick cooking spray and heat over medium heat until hot. Add the onions, garlic, and a dash of salt. Stir to blend. Cover the pan and reduce the heat to low. Cook until the onions have wilted, about 10 minutes. Uncover and continue to cook, stirring occasionally, until the onions are soft and golden brown, 35 to 45 minutes.

Add the tomato paste and cook, stirring, for 1 minute. Stir in the tomatoes, vinegar, and sugar. Reduce the heat to low and cook uncovered, stirring frequently, until the tomatoes have broken down and the mixture has thickened, 45 minutes to 1 hour. Using a handheld immersion blender, puree until smooth. (Alternatively, let cool for 15 minutes. Working in batches, puree the mixture in a blender.) Push the pureed mixture through a food mill or sieve until smooth; discard the solids. Return the strained ketchup to the sauté pan. If the mixture is too thin for ketchup, cook uncovered over low heat until thick. Season to taste with salt and pepper. Let cool completely. Use at once, or refrigerate for up to 3 days. Freeze for longer storage.

5	cups sliced yellow onions
2	tablespoons minced garlic
2	tablespoons tomato paste
2½	cups peeled, seeded, chopped ripe tomatoes, or well-drained canned diced tomatoes
⅓	cup rice vinegar
2	tablespoons turbinado sugar (also known as raw sugar)

Salt
Freshly ground pepper

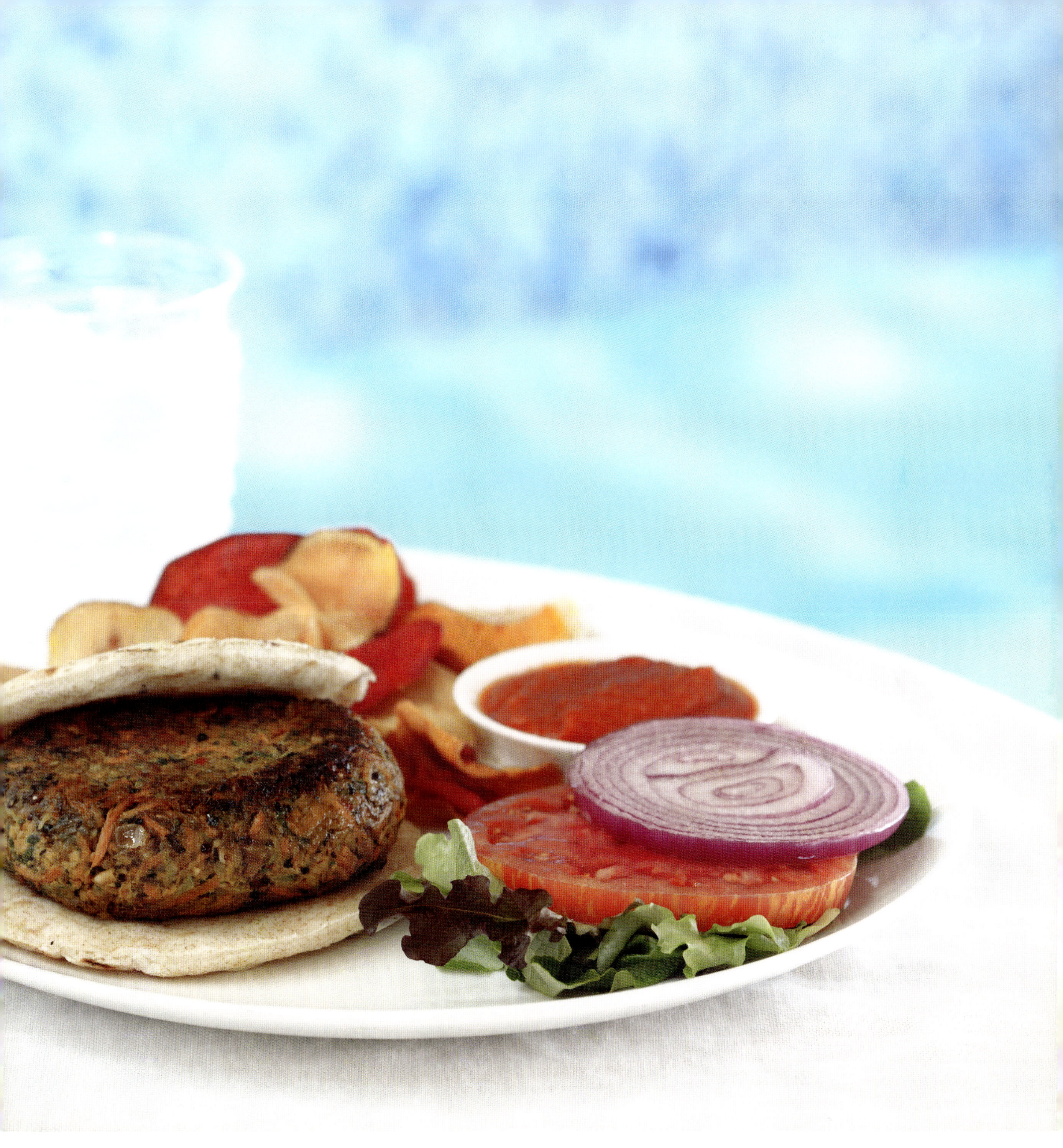

whole wheat–honey flatbread with prosciutto and three-herb pesto /p. 77

Serves 6

We serve this flatbread many different ways—often spread with marinara sauce, cream cheese, or Three-Herb Pesto. Toppings can include just about any vegetable, seafood, or poultry you enjoy. As the final touch, our chefs use a few drops of a special balsamic must imported from Italy, but aged balsamic vinegar will do.

In the bowl of an electric mixer, stir together the warm water and yeast. Let sit until the yeast becomes foamy, about 5 minutes. (If the yeast does not bubble up, discard the mixture and begin again with new yeast.) Add the honey and oil. Using the dough hook attachment, mix until well blended, about 1 minute.

In a medium bowl, combine the flour, semolina, and salt. Whisk gently to blend. With the mixer on low speed, slowly add the flour mixture to the yeast. Increase the speed to medium-high and mix until the dough is smooth and elastic, about 2 minutes. Lightly oil a clean mixing bowl. Add the dough, turning to coat with the oil. Cover with plastic wrap and place in a warm, draft-free spot for 1 hour or until the dough is nicely puffed but not necessarily doubled in bulk.

Preheat the oven to 400°F. Punch down the dough with your fist, and divide it into 6 equal balls, each weighing about 2 ounces. Working 1 at a time on a lightly floured surface, flatten each ball into a circle about ¼ inch thick. Arrange the dough circles on 1 or 2 baking sheets without crowding. Spread 1½ tablespoons of pesto evenly over each flatbread, and top with 3 tomato slices, one slice of the prosciutto and one sixth of the cheese. Bake until the bread is lightly browned and crispy, 7 to 10 minutes. Remove from the oven, sprinkle with a few drops of balsamic vinegar, and serve at once.

Note: A ¼-ounce envelope of active dry yeast contains about 2¼ teaspoons, so you will have some yeast left over.

387 cal, 11 g fat, 22 g prot, 48 g carb

9	tablespoons Three-Herb Pesto (recipe follows)
½	cup warm water (about 110°F)
1½	teaspoons active dry yeast (see Note)
2	tablespoons honey
1	tablespoon extra-virgin olive oil, plus extra for oiling the bowl
1	cup whole wheat flour
¾	cup semolina
½	teaspoon salt
3	ripe tomatoes, sliced (18 slices)
6	very thin slices prosciutto, cut into thin strips
6	tablespoons fresh mozzarella cheese, cut into thin strips

Balsamic must or aged balsamic vinegar

three-herb pesto

Makes about ¾ cup

Fragrant basil is the expected star in pesto, but fresh oregano and parsley add both complexity and balance to this one. A mere ½ teaspoon of cheese and 1½ teaspoons of extra-virgin olive oil are enough to lend that familiar pesto flavor, but it's Mii amo's signature Thickened Vegetable Stock that delivers the silky texture to this all-purpose sauce. And as if that were not enough to change your mind about traditional pesto, our chefs soften the harsh bite of raw garlic by roasting it. You may never return to your old ways.

In a food processor or blender, combine the basil, oregano, parsley, roasted garlic, pumpkin seeds, and Parmesan. Process, pulsing the machine on and off and scraping down the sides of the work bowl as needed, until the herbs are finely chopped. With the machine running, add the stock and oil. If a thinner sauce is desired, add more stock, 1 tablespoon at a time. Season to taste with salt and pepper. Use at once, or refrigerate for up to 2 days. Whisk to blend before using.

6 cloves Roasted Garlic (recipe follows), cooled

¼ cup cooled Thickened Vegetable Stock (recipe follows), or more as needed

1½ cups (lightly packed) fresh basil

¼ cup (lightly packed) fresh oregano

¼ cup (lightly packed) flat-leaf parsley

1½ teaspoons unsalted roasted shelled pumpkin seeds

½ teaspoon freshly grated Parmesan cheese, preferably Parmigiano-Reggiano

1½ teaspoons extra-virgin olive oil

Salt

Freshly ground pepper

roasted garlic

Preheat the oven to 350°F. Put as many whole peeled garlic cloves as you like in a small baking dish or pan. Drizzle with olive oil and toss to coat. Cover the dish with foil and bake until the garlic is very soft when pierced with the tip of a knife, 40 to 50 minutes, depending upon their size. Use at once, or refrigerate, covered, for up to 4 days.

Garlic cloves
Olive oil

thickened vegetable stock

Makes about 4 cups

This variation on our classic vegetarian stock is used frequently in our kitchen, often as an oil replacement in salad dressings and sauces.

Place the cold stock in a medium saucepan. Remove 3 tablespoons of stock from the pan and place it in a small bowl. Add the cornstarch to the bowl and whisk until smooth.

Bring the remaining stock to a boil over high heat. Reduce the heat to medium and whisk in the cornstarch mixture. Cook for 1 minute, whisking until thickened and smooth. Use at once, or cool and refrigerate, covered, for up to 4 days. Before each use, whisk well to blend.

4 cups Vegetable Stock (page 63), chilled

3 tablespoons cornstarch

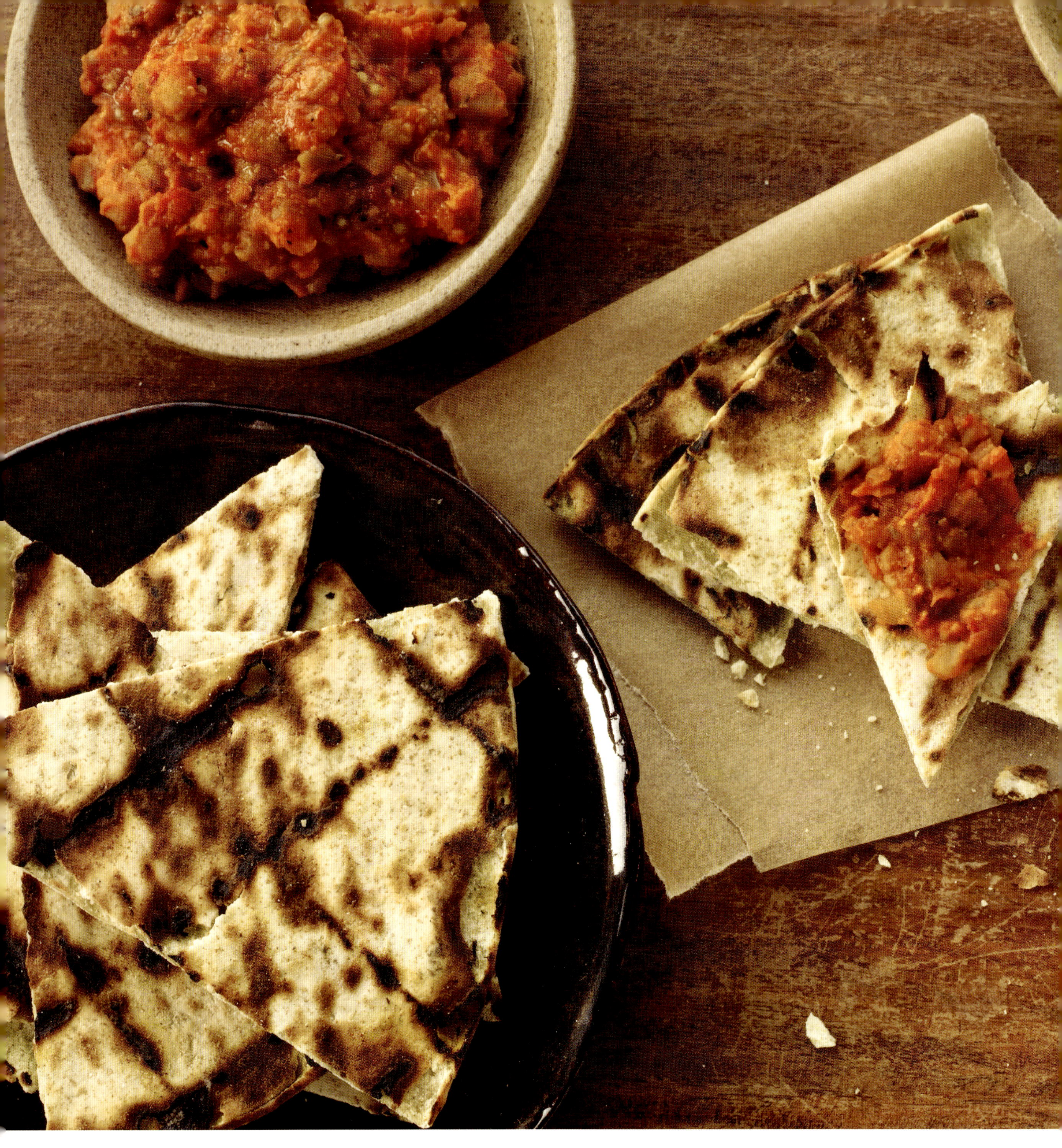

Dinner

artichoke spread

Makes about 2¼ cups, to serve 10

Artichoke dips and spreads are always popular, but many of them are very high in fat. This fiber-rich spread provides all of the flavor without the guilt.

In a medium saucepan, heat the oil over medium heat until hot. Add the onion and garlic and cook, stirring occasionally, until softened, about 3 minutes. Stir in the spinach and season to taste with salt and pepper. Cook just until the spinach is wilted and bright green, about 1 minute. Remove from the heat and set aside to cool.

Place the artichoke hearts in a food processor. Pulse, turning the machine on and off several times, until very coarsely chopped. Add the spinach mixture, cream cheese, herbs, and olives. Pulse several times until well blended. Scrape the mixture into a serving bowl. Serve at once with pita bread, or cover and refrigerate for up to 3 days.

69 cal, 3 g fat, 3 g prot, 7 g carb

1	teaspoon olive oil
½	cup finely chopped onion
3	cloves garlic, minced
1	cup (about 2 ounces) finely chopped fresh spinach
2	cans (13 to 14 ounces each) artichoke hearts, drained
½	cup (4 ounces) fat-free cream cheese, cut into pieces
¼	cup assorted chopped fresh herbs, such as parsley, tarragon, and thyme
¼	cup sliced kalamata olives

Salt
Freshly ground pepper
Fresh or grilled pita bread, for serving

tuscan white bean spread

Makes about 2½ cups, to serve 10

Look for bins of sun-dried tomatoes in the produce section of the supermarket, or in cellophane packages, alongside the canned tomatoes. If you have only oil-packed sun-dried tomatoes in your pantry, blot them dry with paper towels to remove the excess oil, and omit the step of soaking them below.

Place the sun-dried tomatoes in a small heatproof bowl. Add hot water to cover and let stand until soft and pliable, 5 to 10 minutes. Drain well and chop finely. (You should have a little over ¼ cup.)

In a food processor, combine the beans, garlic, oil, lemon juice, ½ teaspoon salt, and freshly ground white pepper, to taste. Process until smooth. Add the sun-dried tomatoes and herbs and process, pulsing the machine on and off, just until blended. Taste, adding more lemon juice, salt, or pepper as needed. Scrape the mixture into a serving bowl. Serve at once with pita bread, or cover and refrigerate for up to 3 days.

112 cal, 1 g fat, 7 g prot, 20 g carb

- 10 sun-dried tomato halves
- 4 cups cooked white beans, or 2 cans (about 15 ounces each) cannellini or other white beans, rinsed and drained
- 3 cloves garlic, minced
- 1¼ teaspoons extra-virgin olive oil
- 1¼ teaspoons fresh lemon juice, or to taste
- ¼ cup minced fresh herbs, such as parsley, basil, and thyme

Salt

Freshly ground white pepper

Fresh or grilled pita bread, for serving

warm crab spread

Makes about 3¼ cups, to serve about 12

This party-sized crab spread is filled with luxurious ingredients, making it one of our most-requested appetizers. You'll need to start by making our special low-fat cream sauce, which gives this spread its silky texture. Refrigerate it while you assemble and prepare the rest of the ingredients.

Preheat the oven to 375°F. In a medium skillet, heat the oil over medium heat until hot. Add the bell peppers, garlic, and jalapeño. Cook, stirring occasionally, until softened, 3 to 5 minutes. Scrape the mixture into the chilled cream sauce. Add the cheese, artichoke hearts, chives, lemon juice, and Worcestershire. Stir to blend. Fold in the crab. Taste, adding more lemon juice if needed. Scrape the mixture into a shallow 1-quart baking dish and bake until bubbly-hot, 25 to 30 minutes. Serve warm with pita bread.

112 cal, 6 g fat, 8 g prot, 5 g carb

- 2 cups Mii amo Cream Sauce (recipe follows), chilled
- 2 teaspoons olive oil
- ½ cup finely chopped red bell pepper
- ½ cup finely chopped green bell pepper
- 2 cloves garlic, minced
- 1 teaspoon minced jalapeño
- 1 cup freshly grated Parmesan cheese
- ½ cup chopped canned artichoke hearts
- ¼ cup chopped fresh chives
- 1 teaspoon fresh lemon juice, or more to taste
- 1 teaspoon Worcestershire sauce
- 4 ounces crabmeat, drained and picked over to remove shells and cartilage

Fresh or grilled pita bread, for serving

mii amo cream sauce

Makes 2½ cups

This sauce can be used for binding purposes for many stuffings, fillings, or other warm dips.

In a medium saucepan, warm the oil over medium heat. Add the garlic and cook, stirring, until it just begins to turn golden, 1 to 1½ minutes. Stir in the milk and cook until hot. Gradually add the cream cheese, whisking gently until melted and smooth. Season with salt and pepper to taste.

In a small bowl, whisk together the cornstarch and water until well blended. Whisk the mixture into the warm cream sauce and let it simmer 1 to 2 minutes, until the mixture is the consistency of mayonnaise. Transfer to a large bowl, and cover and refrigerate until thickened, about 30 minutes.

2 teaspoons olive oil
3 cloves garlic, minced
2 cups nonfat milk
½ cup (4 ounces) fat-free cream cheese, cut into pieces
1½ tablespoons cornstarch
1½ tablespoons water
Salt
Freshly ground pepper

hummus

Makes about 1¾ cups, to serve 8

This Middle Eastern favorite gets a flavor boost from herbs and a hint of cumin. Serve with fresh vegetables and plenty of warm pita bread for dipping.

In a food processor, combine the beans, stock, lemon juice, roasted garlic, oil, tahini, oregano, and cumin. Process until smooth. Season to taste with salt and pepper. Add 2½ teaspoons of the parsley and process just until blended. Scrape the mixture into a serving bowl and garnish with the remaining ½ teaspoon parsley. Serve at once with pita bread, or cover and refrigerate for up to 3 days.

Note: Tahini is available in Middle Eastern markets, health food stores, and many well-stocked supermarkets.

116 cal, 3 g fat, 4 g prot, 18 g carb

- 3 tablespoons Vegetable Stock (page 63) or water
- 2 teaspoons chopped Roasted Garlic (page 78)
- 1 can (about 15 ounces) garbanzo beans or 2 cups cooked garbanzo beans, drained
- 2 teaspoons fresh lemon juice
- 2 teaspoons extra-virgin olive oil
- 1 teaspoon tahini (sesame seed paste; see Note)
- ¼ teaspoon dried oregano
- ⅛ teaspoon ground cumin
- 1 tablespoon chopped fresh parsley

Salt
Freshly ground pepper
Fresh or grilled pita bread, for serving

roasted eggplant and red pepper spread

Makes about 1¼ cups, to serve 4 to 6

These zesty Mediterranean flavors come together with a minimum of fat. This spread has proven to be so popular with our patrons that you may just want to double the recipe for yourself.

Preheat the oven to 350°F. Spray a shallow pan or baking sheet with nonstick cooking spray. Add the eggplant and season with salt and pepper to taste. Drizzle with the oil and toss to coat. Spread the eggplant cubes into an even layer and bake, stirring once or twice, until very soft when pierced with the tip of a knife, about 30 minutes. Set aside to cool.

In a food processor, combine the cooled eggplant, bell pepper, basil, roasted garlic, and vinegar. Process until smooth. Taste, adding additional salt, pepper, or vinegar if needed. Scrape the mixture into a serving bowl. Serve at once with pita bread, or cover and refrigerate for up to 3 days.

51 cal, 2 g fat, 1 g prot, 8 g carb

2 teaspoons chopped Roasted Garlic (page 78)
1 medium eggplant, about 1 pound, peeled and cut into 1-inch cubes
2 teaspoons olive oil
1 roasted red bell pepper, fresh or bottled
2 tablespoons chopped fresh basil
½ teaspoon aged balsamic vinegar, or as needed

Salt
Freshly ground pepper
Fresh or grilled pita bread, for serving

baby beet salad
with tart cherry vinaigrette /p. 90

Serves 4

Dried cherries give spinach a whole new attitude—a play on tart-sweet flavor combinations—made even more dramatic with a mound of lightly dressed beets and a garnish of crisp asparagus spears and silky hearts of palm. As delicious as it is colorful!

Preheat the oven to 375°F. Trim off the beet greens, leaving about 1 inch of the stem attached. (Discard the greens, or save for another use.) Scrub the beets well to clean but do not dry. Place them in a shallow baking dish just large enough to hold them. Drizzle with the oil and season with salt and pepper; toss gently to coat. Cover the dish with foil and bake, shaking the pan every 15 minutes, until the beets are tender when pierced with the tip of a sharp knife, 45 minutes to 1 hour. Let cool.

Working with 1 beet at a time, grasp the beet with a paper towel and slip off the skin. Repeat with the remaining beets. Cut the beets into slices about ⅜ inch thick and toss with ½ cup of the vinaigrette.

Bring a large pot of salted water to a boil over high heat. Add the asparagus. As soon as the water returns to a boil, drain the asparagus in a colander under cold running water until cool. Drain well. Toss the asparagus with 2 tablespoons of the vinaigrette.

In another small bowl, toss the hearts of palm with 2 tablespoons of the vinaigrette.

In a large bowl, toss the spinach with the remaining ¼ cup of the vinaigrette. Divide the spinach equally among 4 to 6 salad plates. Top each with beets and garnish with hearts of palm and asparagus. Sprinkle dried cherries over the top and serve at once.

89 cal, 1 g fat, 5 g prot, 18 g carb

- 1 cup Tart Cherry Vinaigrette (recipe follows), divided
- 2-3 pounds red or gold baby beets, about 1½ inches in diameter
- 1 tablespoon olive oil
- 1 pound asparagus, trimmed
- 1 can (about 14 ounces) hearts of palm, drained, each heart quartered lengthwise
- 6 cups (about 6 ounces) baby spinach
- 1 cup dried tart cherries

Salt

Freshly ground pepper

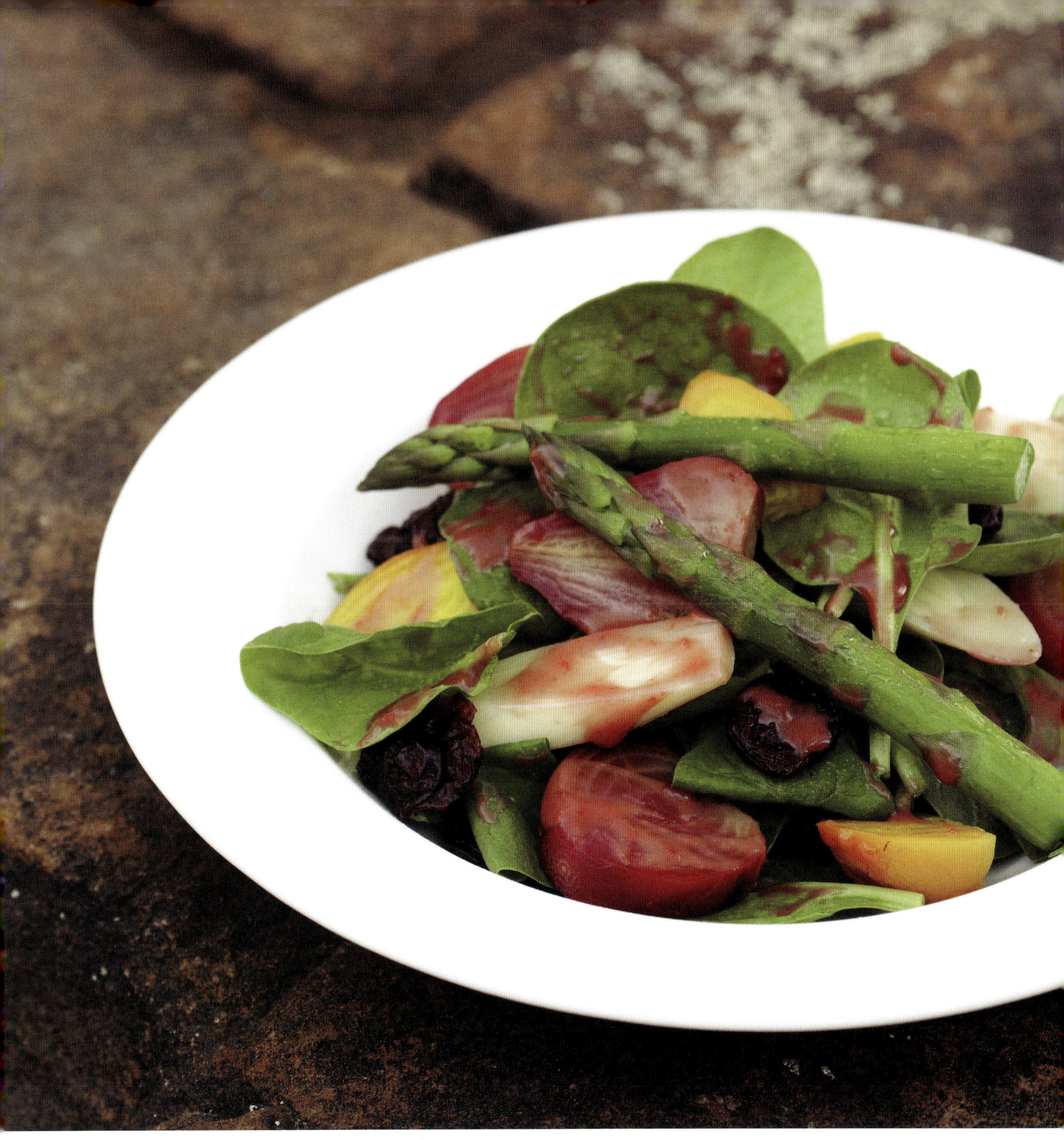

tart cherry vinaigrette

Makes about 1 cup

Place the cherries in a small heatproof bowl. Heat the vinegar in a microwave or small saucepan until hot. Pour over the cherries, tossing to coat, and let stand until cool, about 30 minutes. Puree the cherry mixture in a food processor or blender until smooth. Add the stock and garlic and process until well blended. Season to taste with salt and pepper.

½ cup Thickened Vegetable Stock (page 79)
½ cup dried tart cherries
¼ cup rice wine vinegar
½ teaspoon minced garlic
Salt
Freshly ground pepper

arugula and tomato salad
with basil vinaigrette /p. 92
and balsamic syrup /p. 93

Serves 4

The colors of the Italian flag, paired with the heady aroma of fresh basil, make this salad a feast for the eyes as well as the palate. We like to serve this one in the summer, when vine-ripened tomatoes are at their peak.

In a large bowl, combine the arugula, tomato, onion, and mozzarella. Add the Basil Vinaigrette and toss gently to mix. Divide the salad equally among 4 plates. Drizzle ½ teaspoon of Balsamic Syrup over each salad and serve at once.

158 cal, 9 g fat, 7 g prot, 11 g carb

- ⅓ cup Basil Vinaigrette (recipe follows)
- 2 teaspoons Balsamic Syrup (recipe follows)
- 5 cups (about 5 ounces) baby arugula
- 1 large tomato, seeded and cut into thin strips
- ¼ cup very thinly sliced red onion
- 4 ounces fresh whole-milk mozzarella cheese, cut into thin strips

basil vinaigrette

Makes about ⅓ cup

In a small bowl, whisk together the vinegar, garlic, mustard, and honey. Whisk in the stock and the oil. Cut the basil leaves into very thin slices, or chop finely. Stir them into the dressing. Season to taste with salt and pepper.

3	tablespoons Thickened Vegetable Stock (page 79), whisked until smooth
1	tablespoon white balsamic vinegar
½	teaspoon minced garlic
¼	teaspoon Dijon mustard
¼	teaspoon honey
1½	teaspoons extra-virgin olive oil
6	leaves fresh basil

Salt

Freshly ground pepper

balsamic syrup

Makes about ⅓ cup

This syrup lasts indefinitely in the refrigerator. Bring to room temperature before using. It complements all the spreads in this book, and is also good drizzled on fish, salads, grilled vegetables, and pita bread.

In a small nonstick skillet, bring the vinegar to a boil over medium heat. Let it boil, watching carefully, until reduced by half. Whisk in the corn syrup and continue cooking until it reaches a syrup consistency, about 2 minutes more. Set aside to cool completely.

1 cup balsamic vinegar
2 tablespoons light corn syrup

onion soup

Makes about 8½ cups, to serve 6

To make the bouquet garni for this, you will need a small piece of cheesecloth and about a 6-inch piece of natural cotton butcher's twine. As for the chicken and veal stocks, if you cannot make your own, look for high-quality frozen brands at gourmet shops and upscale supermarkets. The flavor makes all the difference. Like many soups, this one tastes even better the day after it has been made.

To make the bouquet garni, lay a 6-inch square of cheesecloth flat on a work surface. Place the halved garlic cloves, peppercorns, rosemary, and thyme in the center. Bring the 4 corners of the cheesecloth together to enclose the peppercorns and herbs, forming a pouch. Tie securely with twine and set aside.

To make the soup, heat the oil in a soup pot or Dutch oven over medium heat. Stir in the onions, shallots, and minced garlic. Cook covered, lifting the lid 2 or 3 times to stir, until the onions have softened, about 15 minutes. Remove the lid and cook uncovered, stirring occasionally, until the onions are golden brown, 15 to 20 minutes longer. Pour in the brandy, Madeira, and sherry. Increase the heat to high and cook until the liquid is reduced to about ½ cup, 15 minutes. Stir in the thyme and marjoram.

With the heat still on high, add the stocks and bring to a boil. Add the bouquet garni. Reduce the heat to medium and simmer, stirring occasionally, until the flavors have blended and the soup has thickened, 1 hour. Discard the bouquet garni and season the soup to taste with salt and pepper. Serve at once, or cool and refrigerate for up to 3 days. Freeze for longer storage.

160 cal, 1 g fat, 8 g prot, 20 g carb

» Bouquet Garni
2 cloves garlic, halved
3 whole black peppercorns
1 sprig fresh rosemary
1 sprig fresh thyme

» Soup
¾ teaspoon olive or canola oil
4 cups sliced red onions
4 cups sliced yellow onions
2 cups sliced shallots
3 cloves garlic, minced
½ cup brandy
⅓ cup Madeira wine
⅓ cup medium-dry sherry
1¼ teaspoons dried thyme
½ teaspoon dried marjoram
5 cups chicken stock
1 cup veal stock

Salt
Freshly ground pepper

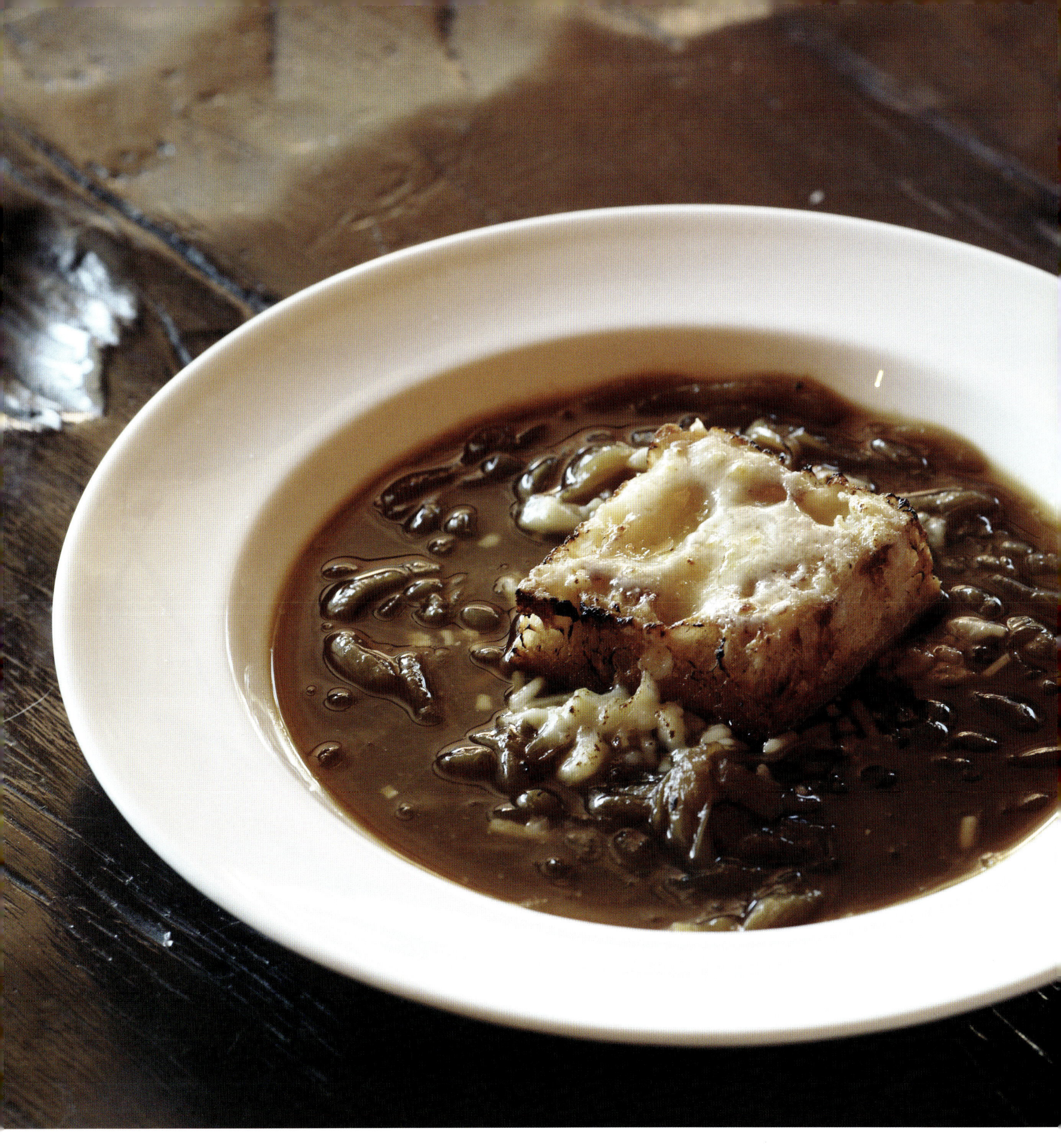

crab and corn cakes
with rémoulade sauce /p. 98

Serves 4

Crab and corn are natural partners, and here they are given a southwestern twist with the addition of chiles and cilantro. In the restaurant we grind our own dried corn, but cornmeal gives a similar result. We serve this popular menu item with our own chunky version of classic French rémoulade sauce.

In a medium skillet or sauté pan, heat the oil over medium heat. Stir in the onion, celery, bell pepper, poblano, and garlic. Reduce the heat to medium-low and cook, stirring occasionally, until softened but not browned, 3 to 5 minutes. Let cool.

Scrape the cooled vegetable mixture into a large bowl. Stir in the egg whites, then mix in the crab, cornmeal, and cilantro until blended. Form the mixture into four 3-inch cakes, each ¾ to 1 inch thick.

Spray a large skillet or griddle with nonstick cooking spray. Heat over medium heat until hot but not smoking. Working in batches if necessary, cook the crab cakes, turning once, until cooked through and lightly browned on the outside, 12 to 14 minutes total. Serve each one warm, with about 2½ tablespoons Rémoulade Sauce on the side.

178 cal, 3 g fat, 16 g prot, 18 g carb

⅔	cup Rémoulade Sauce (recipe follows)
¾	teaspoon olive or canola oil
½	cup minced red onion
6	tablespoons minced celery
¼	cup minced red bell pepper
2	tablespoons minced poblano chile pepper
¾	teaspoon minced garlic
½	cup egg whites
8	ounces Dungeness crabmeat, drained and picked over to remove shells and cartilage
¾	cup yellow cornmeal
1	teaspoon minced fresh cilantro

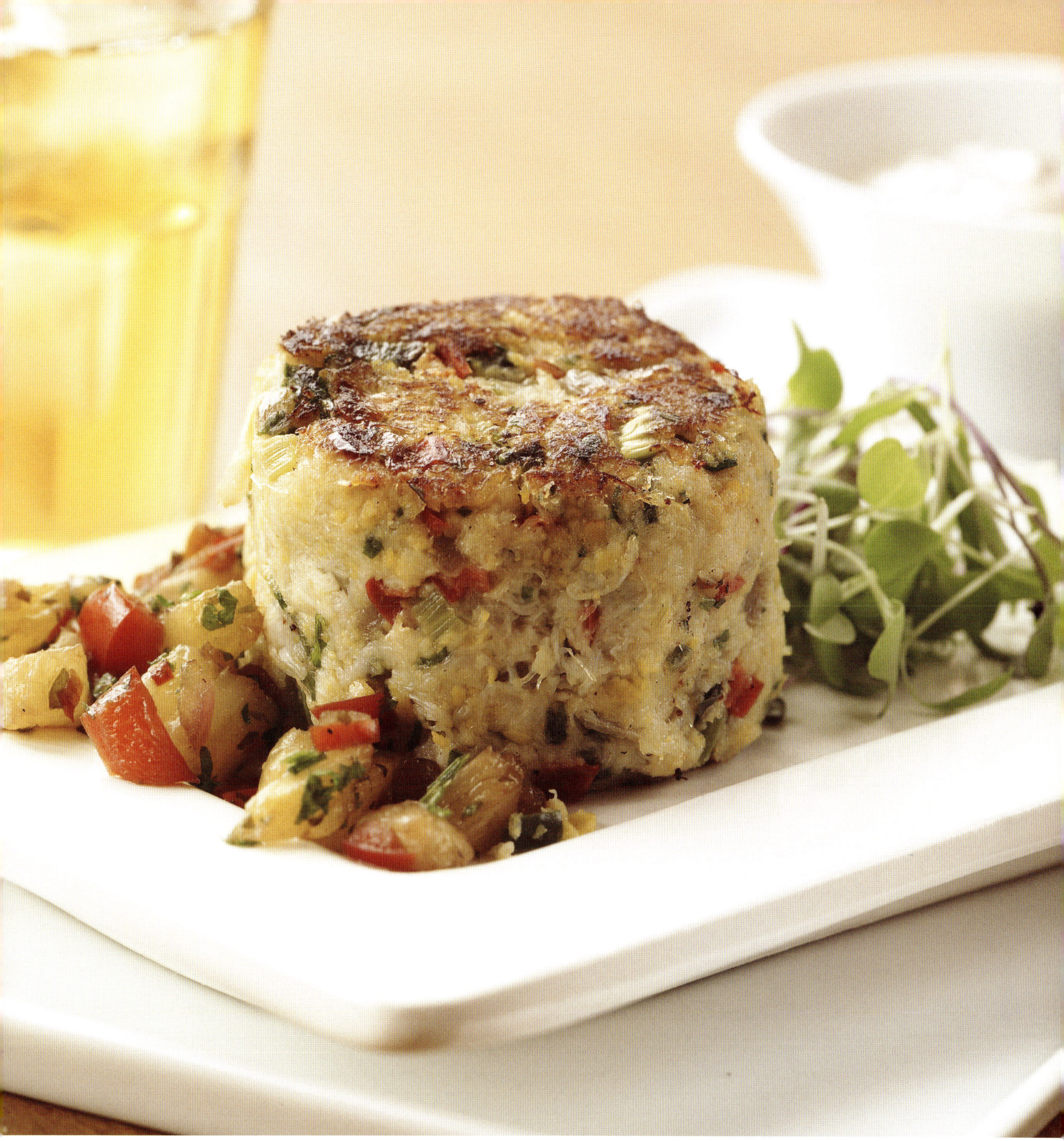

rémoulade sauce

Makes about ⅔ cup

Our chef loves to use Creole mustard. This New Orleans native thinks there is nothing better. If you can't find it though, use a brown mustard.

In a medium bowl, mix together the mayonnaise substitute, pickle, onion, bell pepper, celery, pepperoncini, mustard, cilantro, paprika, horseradish, and garlic. Season to taste with salt and pepper. Use at once, or cover and refrigerate for up to 24 hours.

¼ cup mayonnaise substitute, or nonfat or low-fat mayonnaise
¼ cup minced dill pickle
2 tablespoons minced red onion
2 tablespoons minced red bell pepper
1 tablespoon minced celery
1 tablespoon minced drained pepperoncini
1½ teaspoons Creole mustard
1 teaspoon minced fresh cilantro
¾ teaspoon paprika
¾ teaspoon prepared white horseradish
¼ teaspoon minced garlic

Salt
Freshly ground pepper

shrimp sauté with orzo and vegetables

Serves 4

Like all stir-fry dishes, the secret to success here is having the ingredients prepped and ready to go in the order in which they will be used. Once that is done, the rest of the recipe is simply a flash in the pan.

Preheat the oven to 325°F. Spread the tasso in a single layer on a baking sheet. Bake until browned and crispy at the edges, 10 to 15 minutes.

Bring a medium pot of salted water to a boil over high heat. Add the orzo and cook until tender yet still firm to the bite, 8 to10 minutes. Drain in a colander and rinse with cold running water.

In a large sauté pan, heat the oil over medium heat. Add the onion and garlic and cook, stirring until softened but not browned, 1 to 2 minutes. Increase the heat to medium-high and add the shrimp. Cook, stirring frequently, until the shrimp turn pink on the outside and are just beginning to curl. Pour in the wine and continue cooking until reduced to about 1 tablespoon. Add the tomato, edamame, and stock. Cook, stirring and tossing, until the shrimp are opaque throughout, about 1 minute. Reduce the heat to medium and add the orzo. Cook, stirring, until heated through, 1 to 2 minutes. Season to taste with salt and pepper.

Divide the orzo mixture equally among 4 warmed plates, giving each portion 3 shrimp. Mound the tasso on top of the shrimp and sprinkle the parsley over all. Serve at once.

173 cal, 5 g fat, 22 g prot, 10 g carb

- ½ cup Vegetable Stock (page 63)
- 4 ounces tasso (spicy Cajun-style cured pork), cut into matchstick-sized pieces
- 1 cup uncooked orzo (rice-shaped pasta)
- 1 tablespoon olive oil
- 2 tablespoons minced red onion
- 1 teaspoon minced garlic
- 12 jumbo shrimp (13 to 15 per pound), peeled and deveined, tails off
- ¼ cup Chardonnay or other dry white wine
- 1 medium tomato, seeded and cut into ½-inch dice
- ½ cup fresh or frozen shelled edamame, thawed
- 2 tablespoons minced fresh parsley

Salt

Freshly ground pepper

grilled salmon
with yukon gold potato tart /p. 102
and asparagus-asiago cream /p. 103

Serves 4

The most important thing is to start with the best wild salmon you can find—we use sashimi-grade, the finest quality. In addition to the potatoes, we serve this with a colorful array of seasonal vegetables, such as baby carrots, broccolini, and baby yellow squash.

Spray a grill pan or cast-iron skillet with nonstick cooking spray. Heat over medium-high heat until hot. Rub the salmon all over with the oil and season with salt and pepper. Sprinkle with the herbs, pressing down gently to make them adhere. Grill, turning once, until the salmon is nicely browned on the outside and just barely pink throughout, about 6 minutes total.

Arrange 1 serving of potatoes on each of 4 warmed dinner plates. Place a salmon fillet over the top and drizzle with about 3 tablespoons of Asparagus-Asiago Cream. Serve at once.

342 cal, 14 g fat, 35 g prot, 13 g carb

- 4 pieces Yukon Gold Potato Tart (recipe follows)
- ¾ cup Asparagus-Asiago Cream (recipe follows)
- 4 skinless salmon fillets, each weighing about 4 ounces
- 1 teaspoon olive oil
- 2 tablespoons assorted finely chopped fresh herbs, such as basil, parsley, and chives.

Salt
Freshly ground pepper

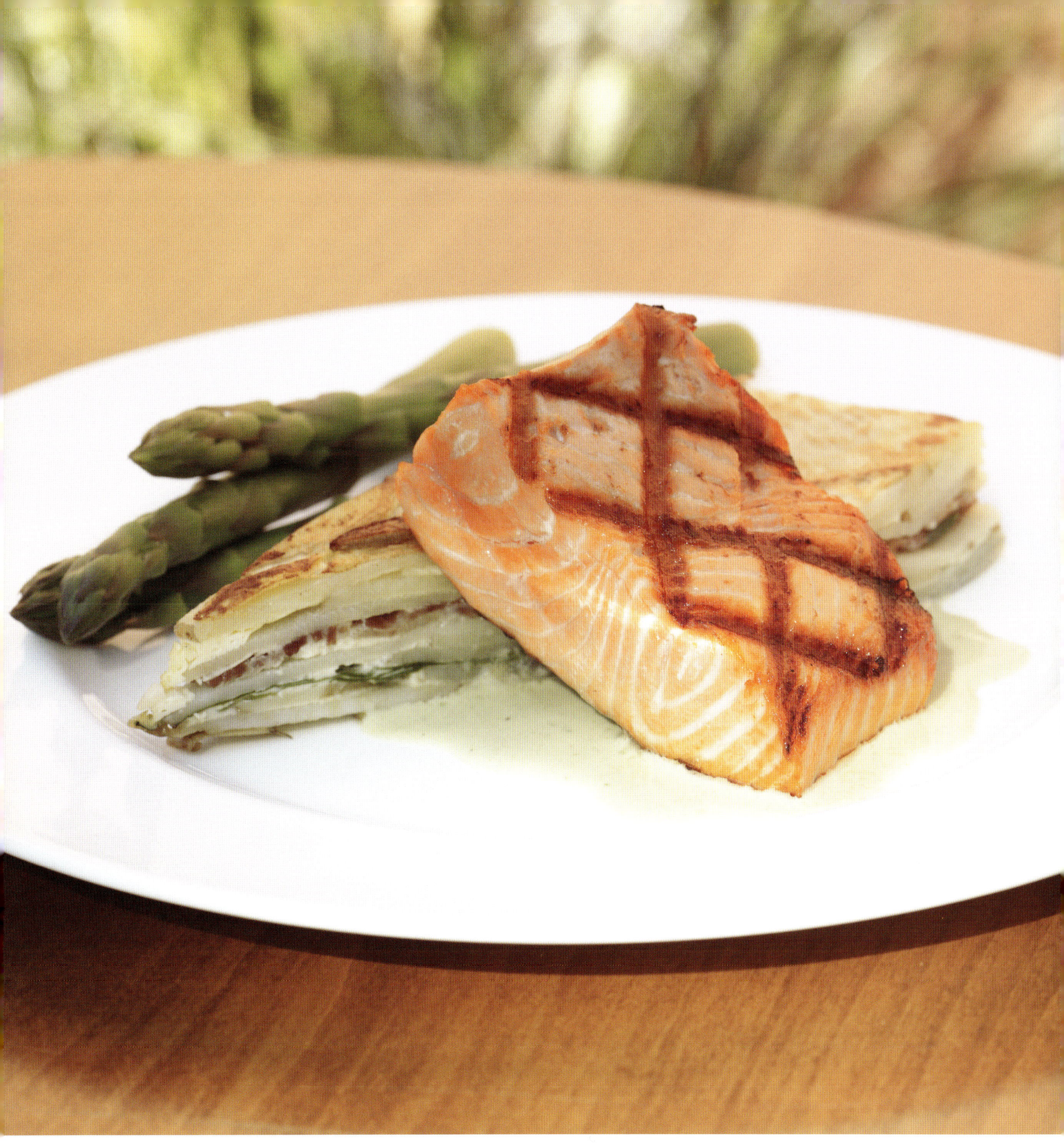

yukon gold potato tart

Makes one 8-inch tart, to serve 10

Preheat the oven to 325°F. Spray an 8-inch round pie or cake pan with nonstick cooking spray. Line the bottom with parchment paper, then spray the paper.

Rinse the spinach thoroughly and drain but do not dry. Put it in a heavy medium saucepan with the water still clinging to its leaves. Season with salt and pepper. Cover and cook over medium heat until the spinach is just wilted, about 1 minute. Drain well, pressing out any liquid from the leaves. Chop coarsely and set aside.

In a medium bowl, combine the half-and-half, egg, and egg white. Season with salt and pepper. Whisk until well blended.

Arrange a single layer of potatoes in the prepared pan, overlapping them slightly. Season with salt and pepper. Scatter a thin layer of chopped spinach over the potatoes, then spoon about 2 tablespoons of the egg mixture over the top. Arrange another layer of overlapping potatoes and season with salt and pepper. Top with an even layer of prosciutto. Continue layering, seasoning the potatoes, and topping with spinach and egg mixture, ending with a layer of potatoes on top.

Bake until the eggs are cooked through and the potatoes are tender when pierced with the tip of a knife, about 30 minutes. To serve, use a 3-inch round cookie cutter to make individual portions, or cut the tart into small squares or thin wedges. (Leftover potatoes can be reheated in a 325°F oven, or served at room temperature alongside a green salad.)

4	cups (about 4 ounces) baby spinach
½	cup fat-free half-and-half or nonfat milk
1	large egg
1	large egg white
1¼	pounds Yukon gold potatoes (about 4), peeled and sliced about ⅛ inch thick
3	very thin slices prosciutto, cut into thin strips

Salt

Freshly ground pepper

asparagus-asiago cream

Makes about ¾ cup

In a medium sauté pan or skillet, heat the oil over low heat until hot. Stir in the asparagus, onion, garlic, and peppercorns. Cook, stirring occasionally, until the asparagus and onion are softened but not browned, 3 to 5 minutes. Increase the heat to medium and stir in the half-and-half. Cook, stirring occasionally, until heated through, 3 to 5 minutes.

In a small bowl, whisk together the cornstarch and water to blend. Stir into the simmering asparagus mixture and cook until slightly thickened, about 2 minutes longer. Stir in the cheese. Season to taste with salt and pepper. Remove from the heat.

Using a handheld immersion blender, puree the mixture until smooth. (Alternatively, let the sauce cool 5 to 10 minutes, then puree in a blender.) Press the mixture through a fine-mesh sieve and discard the solids. Reheat over low heat if needed.

½	teaspoon olive or canola oil
½	cup coarsely chopped asparagus
¼	cup chopped onion
1	small clove garlic, halved
2	whole black peppercorns
¾	cup fat-free half-and-half
½	teaspoon cornstarch
½	teaspoon water
1	tablespoon freshly grated Asiago cheese

Salt
Freshly ground pepper

grilled sea bass
with orzo primavera and saffron broth /p. 106

Serves 4

This colorful entrée is made even more irresistible by a shower of fragrant saffron broth ladled over the top just before serving. The plate is then finished off with steamed broccolini and baby carrots.

Bring a medium pot of salted water to a boil over high heat. Add the orzo and cook until tender yet still firm to the bite, 8 to 10 minutes. Drain in a colander and rinse with cold running water.

In a medium sauté pan, heat 2 teaspoons of the oil over medium heat. Add the onion, celery, carrot, and bell pepper. Cook, stirring, until softened but not browned, about 3 minutes. Stir in the orzo. Cover off the heat to keep warm.

Heat a stovetop grill or cast-iron skillet over medium-high heat until hot. Rub the fish fillets with the remaining 1 teaspoon oil and season with salt and pepper. Cook, turning once, until nicely browned on the outside and just opaque throughout, 6 to 8 minutes total.

Stir the chives into the orzo. Mound one fourth of the orzo in the center of each of 4 warm, large shallow soup bowls or dinner plates. Top each portion with a fillet and drizzle with ¼ cup of the Saffron Broth. Serve at once.

283 cal, 7 g fat, 25 g prot, 23 g carb

- 1 cup Saffron Broth (recipe follows)
- 1 cup uncooked orzo (rice-shaped pasta)
- 3 teaspoons olive oil, divided
- 3 tablespoons finely chopped red onion
- 1 tablespoon finely chopped celery
- 1 tablespoon finely chopped carrot
- 1 tablespoon finely chopped red bell pepper
- 4 sea bass or other firm-fleshed white fish fillets, about 4 ounces each
- 1½ tablespoons thinly sliced fresh chives

Salt
Freshly ground pepper

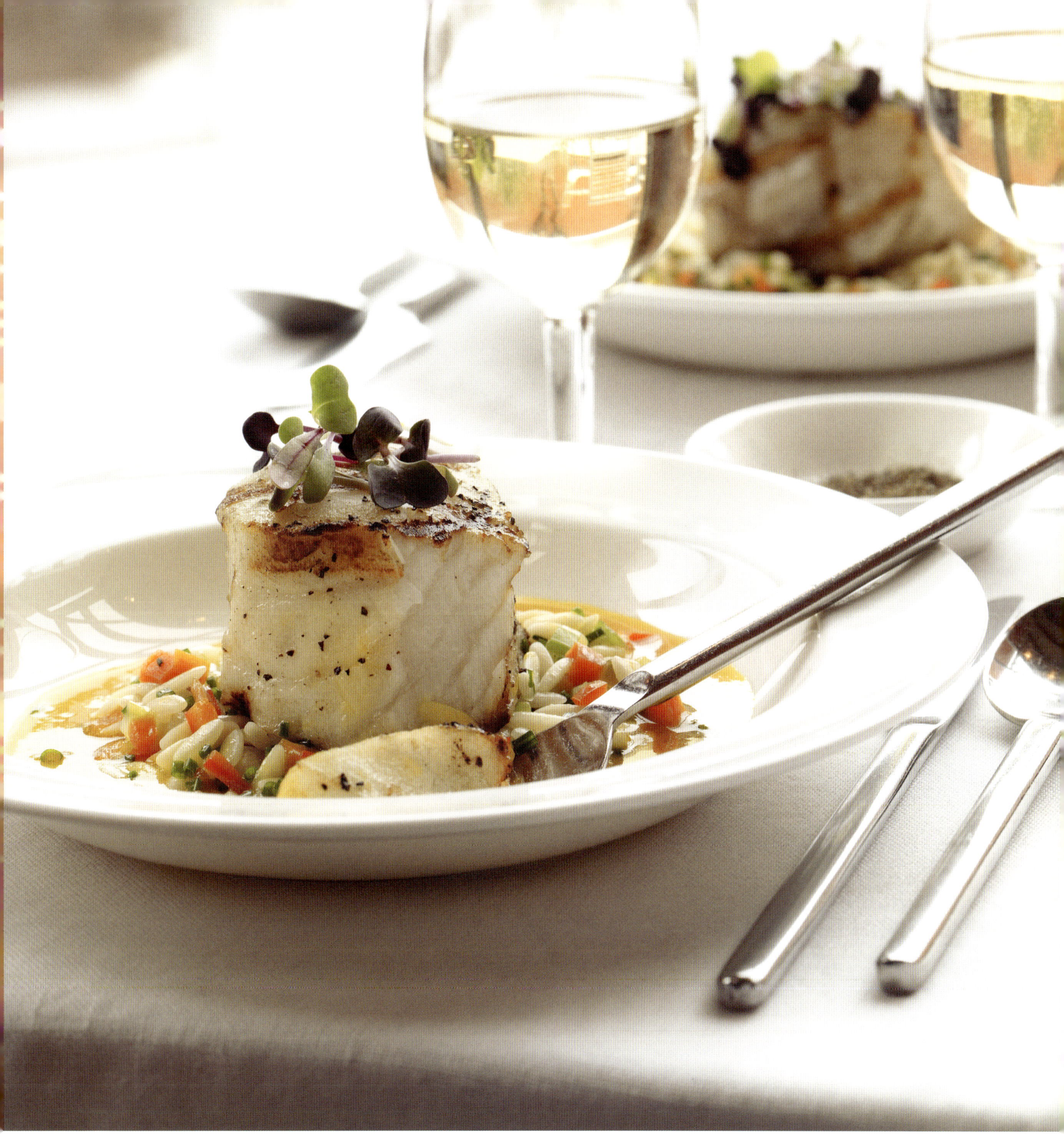

saffron broth

Makes about 1 cup

Saffron is oil soluble, so cooking it a bit before adding it to a liquid helps release some of the flavor.

Spray a medium skillet with nonstick cooking spray. Heat over medium heat until hot. Add the mushrooms, shallot, garlic, and saffron and cook until softened, 2 to 3 minutes. Stir in the potato. Pour in the wine and cook until reduced to about ¼ cup, 3 to 5 minutes. Stir in the stock and increase the heat to medium-high. Cook until the stock has thickened slightly and reduced by half, 5 to 7 minutes.

Using a handheld immersion blender, puree the mixture until smooth. (Alternatively, let the sauce cool 5 to 10 minutes, then puree in a blender or food processor.) Strain the mixture through a sieve and discard the solids. Season to taste with salt and pepper.

1½ cups Vegetable Stock (page 63)
2 cremini mushrooms, chopped
1 tablespoon chopped shallot
¼ teaspoon minced garlic
½ teaspoon saffron threads
2 tablespoons peeled and chopped Yukon gold potato
¾ cup dry white wine
Salt
Freshly ground pepper

herb-crusted colorado lamb
with rosemary jus /p. 108

Serves 4

Our chefs trim away most of the fat to expose the tender meat, but you can have your butcher cut the lamb into the smaller portions needed for this recipe, and trim and "french" the racks to expose the bones and remove excess fat. We use our own blend of fresh rosemary, thyme, parsley, and lavender for seasoning. If you don't have an herb garden at home, you can get similar results with herbes de Provence, a dried blend available at gourmet shops and many well-stocked supermarkets. We serve this with tiny steamed carrots and baby zucchini.

Preheat the oven to 475°F. Rinse the spinach thoroughly and drain but do not dry. In a medium skillet, preferably nonstick, warm 1 teaspoon of the oil over medium heat until hot. Add the spinach with the water still clinging to its leaves. Season with salt and pepper. Cook, stirring, until the spinach is just wilted, about 1 minute. Stir in the beans and tomato and keep warm off the heat.

Rub the lamb racks with the remaining 1 teaspoon oil and season with salt and pepper. Rub each of the racks with 1 teaspoon of herbs, pressing in gently to make them adhere. Spray a cast-iron skillet or other heavy pan with nonstick cooking spray. Heat over high heat until hot. Working in batches if necessary, cook the racks, turning several times, until browned all over, 3 to 5 minutes total. In the same skillet or a roasting pan, lay the racks bone-side down without crowding. Roast in the oven until the lamb reaches the desired doneness, 10 to 15 minutes for medium-rare (130° to 140°F). Let the racks rest on a cutting board for 5 minutes before slicing into individual rib chops.

Mound one fourth of the bean mixture in the center of each of 4 warmed, large shallow soup bowls or plates. Top each with 3 rib chops and drizzle with about 3 tablespoons of Rosemary Jus. Serve at once.

349 cal, 11 g fat, 36 g prot, 24 g carb

¾ cup Rosemary Jus (recipe follows)
2 cups (about 2 ounces) baby spinach
2 teaspoons olive oil, divided
2 cups (about one 15-ounce can) cooked white beans, such as cannellini, drained
¼ cup finely chopped seeded tomato
4 well-trimmed racks of lamb, each weighing about 6 ounces (about 3 ribs each)
4 teaspoons herbes de Provence

Salt

Freshly ground pepper

rosemary jus

Makes about ¾ cup

Spray a small skillet with nonstick cooking spray and heat over medium heat. Add the shallot and garlic and cook until fragrant, about 1 minute. Stir in the tomato paste. Add the rosemary, thyme, and bay leaf. Pour in the wine and increase the heat to medium-high. Cook until it is reduced to about ¼ cup, 2 to 3 minutes. Add the stock and cook until the volume has reduced by half, about 5 minutes. Strain the mixture through a sieve and discard the solids. Keep warm.

2	tablespoons chopped shallot
1	small clove garlic, halved
1	teaspoon tomato paste
1	sprig fresh rosemary
1	small sprig fresh thyme
1	small bay leaf
½	cup dry white wine
1	cup veal or chicken stock

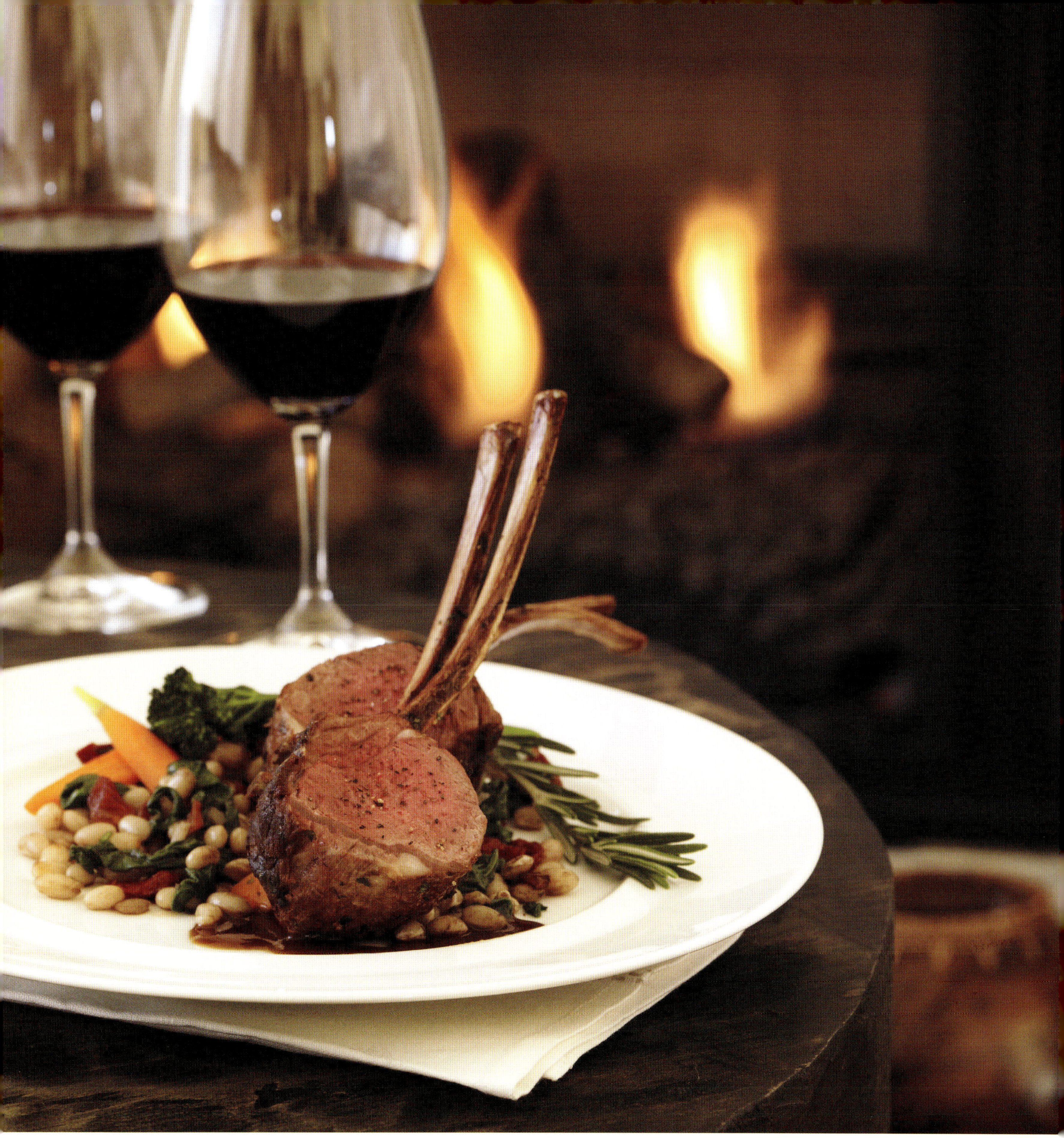

filet mignon with truffled peruvian potatoes
and wild mushroom demi-glace /p.111

Serves 4

Our chefs believe that special ingredients deserve a dramatic presentation, so this meltingly tender steak is served atop a mound of truffle-flecked blue potatoes. The plate then receives an edible garnish of steamed fresh asparagus and baby carrots.

Put the potatoes in a large saucepan. Add enough cold water to cover by 1 inch and season with salt. Cover and bring to a boil over high heat. Reduce the heat to medium-high and boil until the potatoes are very tender when pierced with the tip of a knife, about 15 minutes. Drain. When cool enough to handle, peel the potatoes and place them in a large bowl. Add the sour cream and mash until smooth. Mix in the chopped truffle, truffle oil, and parsley. Season with salt and pepper to taste. Keep warm.

Heat a stovetop grill pan or cast-iron skillet over high heat until hot. Rub the steaks all over with the canola oil and season with salt and pepper. Working in batches if necessary, grill the steaks without crowding, turning once, just until nicely browned on both sides. Reduce the heat to medium and continue cooking, turning once, until the steaks are cooked to the desired doneness, about 8 minutes for medium-rare. Transfer to a cutting board and let rest 5 minutes.

Place a small mound of potatoes in the center of each of 4 warmed dinner plates. Place a filet on top of each and drizzle with about 3 tablespoons of Wild Mushroom Demi-Glace. Serve at once.

321 cal, 9 g fat, 29 g prot, 23 g carb

- ¾ cup Wild Mushroom Demi-Glace (recipe follows)
- 1 pound Peruvian blue potatoes or other boiling potatoes
- 1 teaspoon nonfat sour cream
- 4 teaspoons finely chopped drained canned truffle peelings
- 1 teaspoon white truffle oil
- 4 teaspoons finely chopped fresh parsley
- 4 filet mignon (beef tenderloin) steaks, cut ¾ to 1 inch thick, each weighing about 4 ounces
- 2 teaspoons canola oil

Salt

Freshly ground pepper

wild mushroom demi-glace

Makes about ¾ cup

Place the dried mushrooms in a small bowl and cover with ¼ cup of hot tap water. Let sit until the mushrooms are softened and rehydrated, about 15 minutes. Strain the mushroom broth through a fine-mesh sieve into a small bowl; reserve. Chop the mushrooms coarsely.

Heat the oil in a medium skillet over medium heat. Add the rehydrated dried mushrooms, the fresh mushrooms, and the shallot. Cook, stirring occasionally, until the mushroom liquid has exuded and then evaporated, about 3 minutes. Add the wine, brandy, and thyme and cook, stirring occasionally, until only about 2 tablespoons of liquid remain in the pan.

In a small bowl, whisk the cornstarch into 1 tablespoon of the cold stock until smooth.

Pour the reserved mushroom broth and the remaining stock into the mushroom mixture. Increase the heat to high and cook until the liquid has thickened and reduced by one third, 3 to 5 minutes. Cook over medium heat until bubbles appear around the edge of the pan. Whisk in the cornstarch mixture and cook until thickened, about 1 minute longer. Season to taste with salt and pepper. Use at once, or refrigerate for up to 3 days. Reheat gently before using.

¼ ounce (about 6) dried morel mushrooms
1 teaspoon olive oil
2 oyster mushrooms, chopped
2 shiitake mushrooms, chopped
3 cremini mushrooms, chopped
1 small shallot, chopped
¼ cup dry red wine
2 tablespoons brandy
½ teaspoon chopped fresh thyme
1 teaspoon cornstarch
1 cup veal or beef stock, chilled
Salt
Freshly ground pepper

buffalo tenderloin with horseradish potato cake and chipotle-tomato jus /p.114

Serves 4

Buffalo meat, which is naturally low in fat and calories, is becoming increasingly popular. Most people are pleasantly surprised at its clean, mild flavor. We cold-smoke the tenderloins here at Mii amo. If you have the necessary equipment, you may want to do the same at home; otherwise, simply grill plain tenderloin steaks as directed. We usually round out each plate with a serving of colorful baby carrots and broccolini. The final drizzle of jus gets a surprising jolt of flavor from chipotle chile, a smoked jalapeño. Look for them in small cans at Latin markets and in the Mexican foods section of many supermarkets. When refrigerated in an airtight jar, the leftover chiles will last almost indefinitely.

Preheat the oven to 400°F. Pierce the potatoes several times with a fork. Place them on the oven rack and bake until the potatoes are tender when pierced with the tip of a knife, 45 minutes to 1 hour, depending upon their shape. When cool enough to handle, cut the potatoes in half. Use a spoon to scoop the white flesh into a bowl. Discard the potato skins, or reserve for another use. Add the horseradish, milk, and cheese to the potatoes. Season with salt and pepper to taste, and mash with a fork until nearly smooth. Mix in the chives. Form the potatoes into 4 equal patties, each about ½ inch thick.

Warm 2 tablespoons of the oil in a large nonstick skillet over medium heat until hot. Working in batches if necessary, cook the potato cakes without crowding, turning once, until nicely browned on the outside and heated through, 7 to 10 minutes total. Keep warm.

Cut the tenderloin crosswise into four 4-ounce filets. Rub the filets all over with the remaining 2 tablespoons oil and season with salt and pepper. Preheat a grill pan or cast-iron skillet over medium-high heat until hot. Grill, turning once or twice, until nicely browned on the outside but still pink and juicy inside, 7 to 10 minutes total. Let the meat rest 5 minutes before serving.

Place 1 potato cake in the center of each of 4 warmed, shallow soup bowls or dinner plates. Top each with a buffalo filet and drizzle with 3 tablespoons of Chipotle-Tomato Jus.

403 cal, 15 g fat, 30 g prot, 33 g carb

- ¾ cup Chipotle-Tomato Jus (recipe follows)
- 2 large russet potatoes (about 1 pound total)
- 1 tablespoon prepared white horseradish
- 1 tablespoon nonfat milk
- 1 teaspoon freshly grated Parmesan cheese, preferably Parmigiano-Reggiano
- 1 tablespoon thinly sliced fresh chives
- 4 tablespoons olive oil, divided
- 1 pound buffalo tenderloin

Salt
Freshly ground pepper

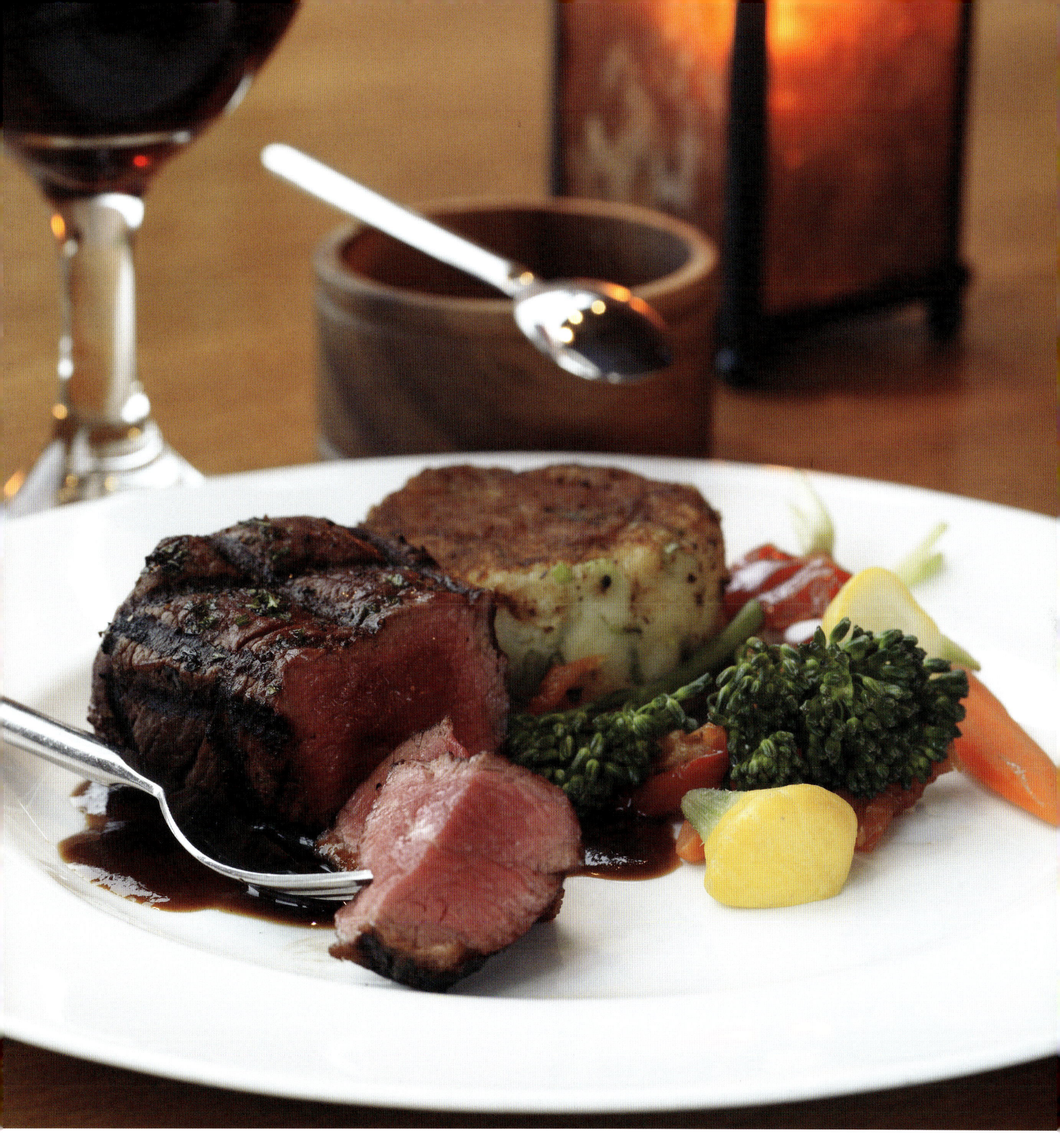

chipotle-tomato jus

Makes about ¾ cup

Spray a skillet with nonstick cooking spray. Heat over medium heat until hot. Add the shallot, tomato, cilantro, garlic, chipotle, and tomato paste. Cook, stirring occasionally, until the vegetables are softened, about 3 minutes.

Add the wine, thyme, and bay leaf. Increase the heat to high. Cook, stirring occasionally, until the liquid has reduced to about ¼ cup, 5 to 7 minutes. Add the stock and continue cooking over high heat until the liquid has thickened and reduced to about ¾ cup, 7 to 10 minutes more. Strain the jus through a sieve and discard the solids. Season with salt and pepper to taste. Use at once, or cover and refrigerate for up to 3 days; freeze for longer storage. Reheat gently before using.

1	tablespoon chopped shallot
1	tablespoon finely chopped tomato
2	teaspoons minced fresh cilantro
1	clove garlic, halved
1	teaspoon minced canned chipotle chile in adobo sauce
½	teaspoon tomato paste
1	cup dry red wine
1	small sprig fresh thyme
1	small bay leaf
2	cups veal or beef stock

Salt
Freshly ground pepper

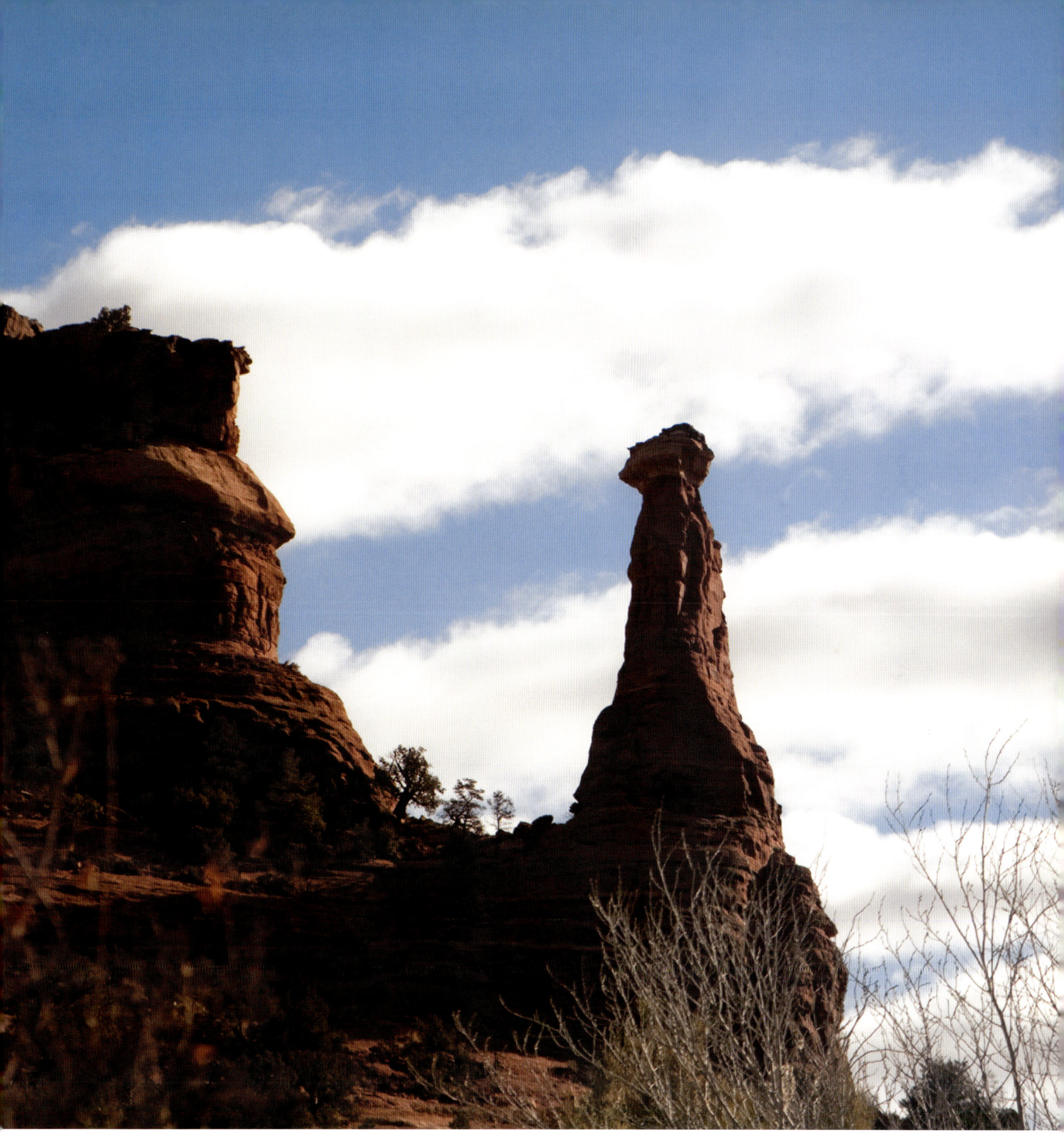

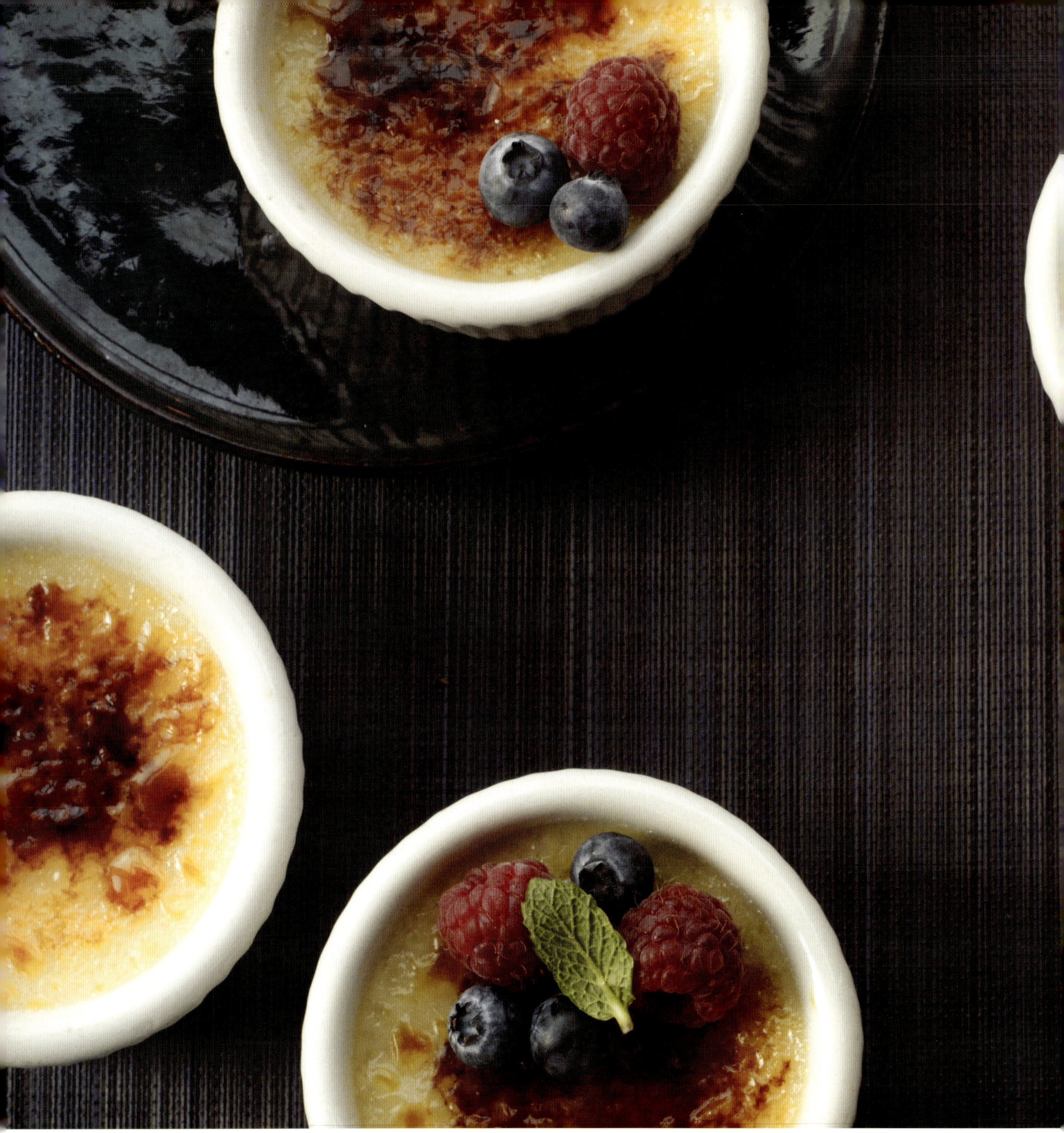

Dessert

berry martini

Serves 4

Here's a martini you can eat with a spoon—with no chance of a hangover! In reality, the only thing martini-esque about this is the glass, but the presentation is definitely enough to make our guests sit up and take notice . . . and hope for another round. Look for sweet-tart fig-balsamic vinegar in gourmet shops and upscale supermarkets. One taste, and you'll never want to be without it in your pantry.

In a large bowl, gently whisk together the yogurt and honey until well blended. Fold in the berries. Divide the mixture equally among 4 martini glasses, mounding the tops slightly. Drizzle each with 1 teaspoon of vinegar and garnish with a mint sprig. Serve at once.

179 cal, 2 g fat, 6 g prot, 36 g carb

- 3 cups nonfat plain yogurt
- 3 tablespoons honey
- 4 cups mixed fresh berries, such as strawberries, hulled and quartered, raspberries, and blueberries
- 4 teaspoons fig-balsamic vinegar
- 4 small fresh mint sprigs, for garnish

peach-blueberry crisp

Serves 6

Everyone enjoys having their own personal dessert—especially when it involves juicy spiced peaches and blueberries. Serve these crisps warm and fragrant from the oven, unadorned or topped with a small scoop of your favorite sorbet. The addition of cardamom brings out the flavor of the peaches in this recipe.

To make the crisps: In a medium saucepan, combine the honey, arrowroot, lemon juice, almond extract, cinnamon, cardamom, and salt. Stir until well blended. Add the peaches, tossing gently to coat. Cook uncovered over medium heat, stirring occasionally, until the peaches are tender and the juices have thickened, about 20 minutes. Stir in the blueberries and cook 5 minutes longer. Divide the mixture equally between six 6-ounce custard cups or ramekins. Set aside at room temperature while you make the topping. If making these ahead, cover and refrigerate them for up to 48 hours. Allow them to come to room temperature before adding the topping (otherwise they will still be cold in the center when topping is cooked).

Preheat the oven to 325°F. Line a baking sheet with foil and spray it with nonstick cooking spray. In a medium bowl, combine the oats, flour, and salt. Toss gently to blend. Add the oil and syrup, stirring until the dry ingredients are evenly moistened. Spread the mixture in an even layer on the prepared baking sheet. Bake until lightly toasted and fragrant, 10 to 15 minutes. Let cool. (If you plan to serve the crisps soon, do not turn off the oven.)

To serve the crisps, preheat the oven to 325°F. Shortly before serving, sprinkle about 1 tablespoon of the topping over each crisp. Bake until the filling is bubbly hot and the topping is crisp and golden, about 15 minutes. Serve warm.

Note: We use arrowroot instead of cornstarch to help thicken the juice because cornstarch would turn the liquid cloudy and cause it to congeal in the refrigerator.

154 cal, 3 g fat, 2 g prot, 33 g carb

» Crisps
- ¼ cup honey
- 1½ tablespoons arrowroot (see Note)
- 1½ teaspoons fresh lemon juice
- ½ teaspoon almond extract
- ¼ teaspoon ground cinnamon
- ¼ teaspoon ground cardamom
- 4 medium peaches (about 1 pound), peeled and sliced, or 3 cups frozen sliced peaches, thawed
- 1 cup (6 ounces) fresh or frozen blueberries
- Dash of salt

» Topping
- 6 tablespoons old-fashioned rolled oats, such as Quaker Oats
- 2 tablespoons whole wheat flour
- 2¼ teaspoons canola oil
- 2¼ teaspoons brown rice syrup or honey
- Dash of salt

fresh fruit tart

Makes one 9-inch tart, to serve 6

Our chefs usually serve individual fruit tarts to our guests, but home cooks may find it easier to make one large tart. The recipes for the pastry and luscious filling remain the same throughout the year, but the colorful fruit display on top changes with the seasons. Brown rice syrup is a substitute for honey. Look for it in natural foods stores or in well-stocked supermarkets.

To make the tart shell: Preheat the oven to 375°F. In a food processor, combine the flour and salt. Pulse the machine on and off once or twice to blend. Add the syrup, apple juice, and oil and process, pulsing the machine on and off, just until the dough forms a cohesive mass. Press the dough evenly into a 9-inch tart pan with a removable bottom. (Alternatively, the dough can be divided equally between four 4-inch tart pans.) Weight the crust with pie weights or prick it to prevent puffing. Bake until the crust is lightly browned and cooked through, 25 to 30 minutes (or 15 to 20 minutes for individual tarts). Cool the crust in the pan on a wire rack for 10 minutes; then carefully remove the edge of the tart pan and let the crust cool completely.

To make the filling: In a large bowl, whisk together the eggs, sugar, and cornstarch until well blended. Pour the milk into a medium saucepan. Use a small sharp knife to cut the vanilla bean in half lengthwise. Use the tip of the knife to scrape the vanilla bean seeds into the milk; then add the halved vanilla bean for extra flavor. Cook over medium heat just until bubbles appear around the edge of the pan. Remove the vanilla bean pods (see Note). Whisk about ½ cup of the hot milk into the egg mixture, then whisk in the remaining milk to blend well. Return the mixture to the saucepan and cook over medium heat, whisking frequently, until thick—similar to the consistency of cold pudding. Pour the custard into a shallow pan or dish, let cool completely, then spread it evenly in the cooled tart shell(s).

Arrange fruit decoratively on top. Serve at once, or cover and refrigerate for up to 6 hours. (If making in advance, avoid using fruit that discolors quickly, such as bananas and apples.)

Note: Used vanilla bean pods may be rinsed, patted dry with paper towels, and left at room temperature to dry completely. Place the dried pods inside an airtight container filled with granulated sugar, to infuse the sugar with vanilla fragrance.

480 cal, 15 g fat, 12 g prot, 73 g carb

» Tart Shell
1½ cups all-purpose flour
¼ cup brown rice syrup
¼ cup apple juice
¼ cup canola oil
   Dash of salt

» Pastry Cream Filling
4 large eggs
½ cup sugar
¼ cup cornstarch
2 cups nonfat milk
1 vanilla bean

4 cups fresh seasonal fruit, such as sliced peaches or nectarines, strawberries, raspberries, blueberries, blackberries, sliced kiwi, and bananas

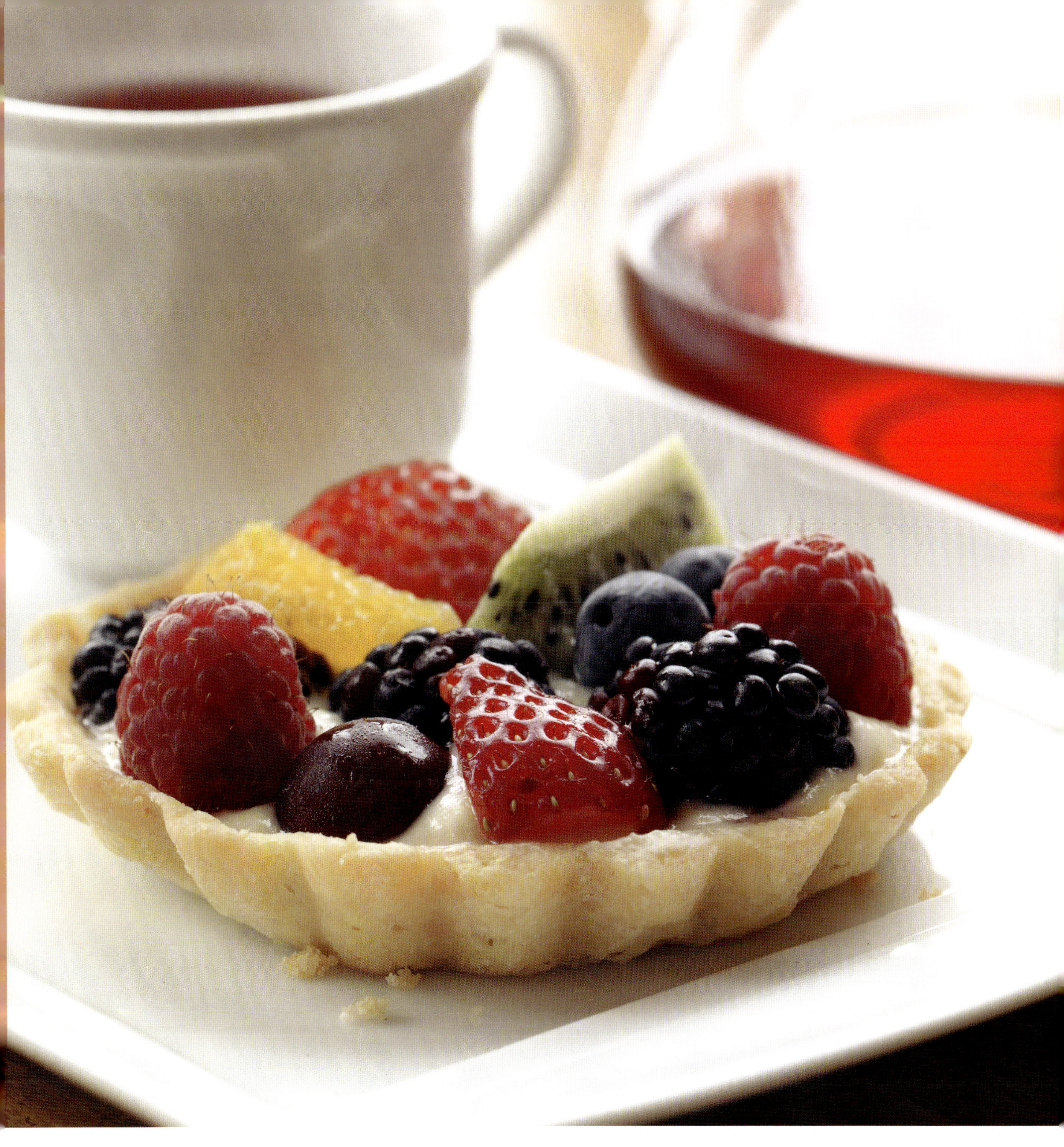

cherry-apple strudel

Makes one 12-inch strudel, to serve 8

Phyllo dough becomes dry and brittle when exposed to air, so it is important to work quickly, and to keep any unused sheets of dough covered with plastic wrap. There are usually about 20 sheets of phyllo in a box, so wrap the remainder airtight and freeze for another time.

Preheat the oven to 350°F. Line a baking sheet with parchment paper or spray with nonstick cooking spray. In a large bowl, combine the apples, cherries, sugar, lemon juice, flour, cinnamon, and allspice. Toss gently to blend.

Remove the phyllo dough from the box, unfold, and lift off 4 sheets from the stack. Cover the sheets with plastic wrap, then lay a damp tea towel over the plastic. Place 1 sheet of the phyllo flat on a work surface, with the long side facing you. Spray it completely with nonstick cooking spray and top with another sheet, aligning the corners as much as possible, and spray that with nonstick cooking spray. Repeat with the remaining 2 sheets of dough. Spoon the apple mixture across the length of the phyllo, on the lower third closest to you, about 2 inches from the bottom, forming a 3-inch wide strip of filling. Leave a 2- to 3-inch border uncovered at either end of the dough. Gently lift the edge of dough closest to you and lay it over the filling. Fold in both of the ends to enclose the filling completely. Roll the stack away from you, forming a tight cylinder. Carefully place the strudel, seam-side down, on the prepared baking sheet. Spray it all over with nonstick cooking spray. Bake until the filling is bubbly-hot and the pastry is crisp and golden, about 30 minutes. Let cool on the baking sheet for at least 10 minutes. Cut the strudel diagonally into slices about 1½ inches thick and dust them lightly with confectioners' sugar.

104 cal, 1 g fat, 1 g prot, 26 g carb

- 2 cups peeled, cored, and chopped tart green apples, such as Granny Smith (about 2 large)
- ½ cup dried tart cherries
- 6 tablespoons (packed) light brown sugar
- 1½ teaspoons fresh lemon juice
- 1½ teaspoons all-purpose flour
- ½ teaspoon ground cinnamon
- ½ teaspoon ground allspice
- 4 sheets (each about 18 x 14 inches) frozen phyllo dough, thawed as package directs

Nonstick cooking spray
Confectioners' (powdered) sugar

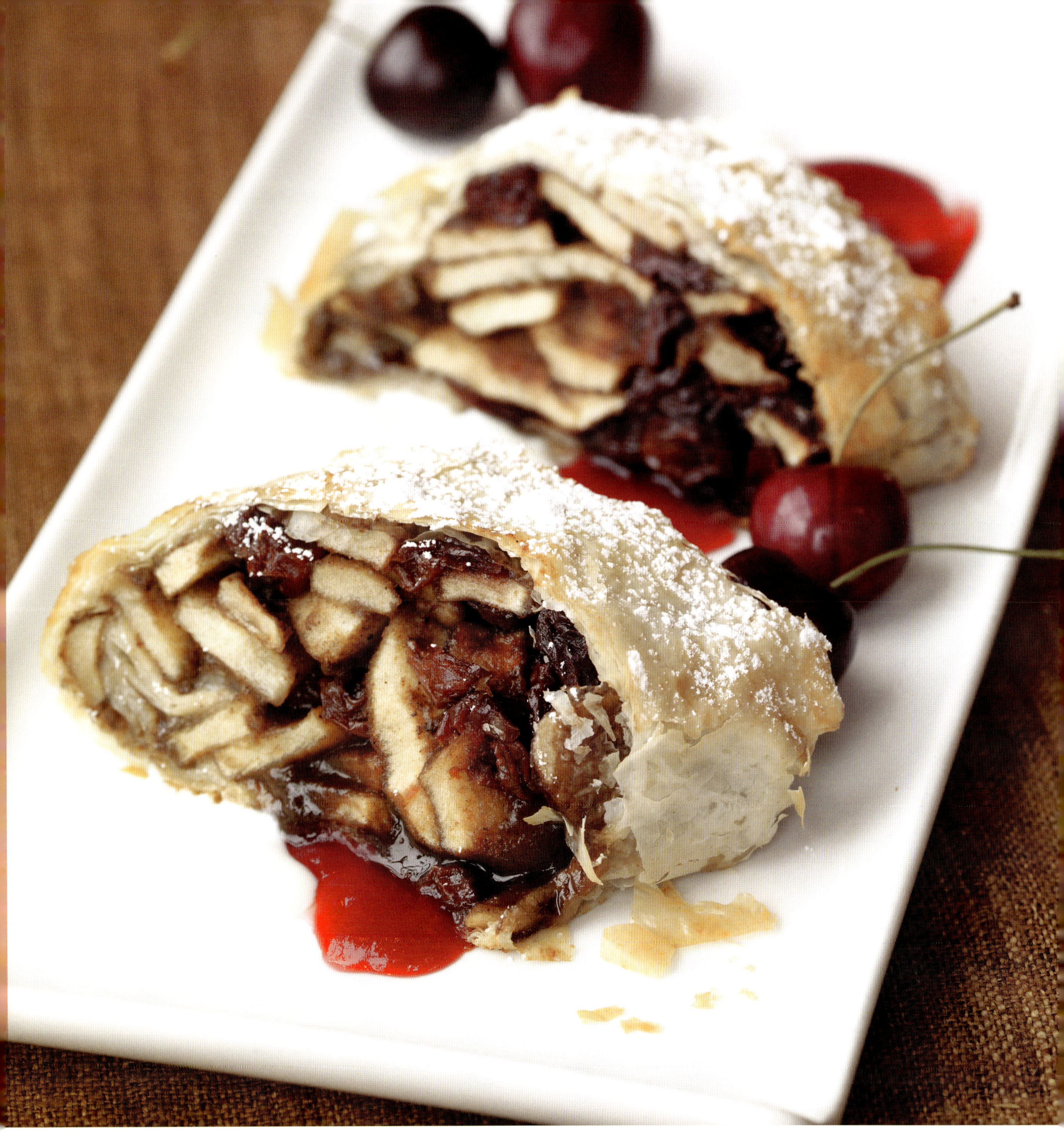

fruit sorbet

Makes about 3 cups, to serve 6

Frozen desserts are always a special treat, but serving a colorful trio of brilliantly flavored sorbets is downright magical. Here at Mii amo we puree fresh seasonal fruits, but frozen fruit will do in a pinch. Try for unique flavor combinations of varying colors, such as black currant, guava, and raspberry. If making more than one sorbet, plan ahead accordingly. Because this contains no stabilizers, it is best eaten within a day or two. Alcohol is used as a stabilizer here to prevent the sorbet from freezing too hard. The alcohol also helps to keep the sorbet for longer periods of time in the freezer without turning to ice. If you prefer to not use alcohol, eat the sorbet as soon as it freezes.

In a medium saucepan, cook the fruit juice over high heat until it is reduced to about 1 cup, 8 to 10 minutes. Let cool to room temperature. Mix the reduced fruit juice with the fruit puree and vodka. Cover and refrigerate until cold, at least 4 hours or overnight.

Pour the mixture into the canister of an ice cream maker and freeze according to the manufacturer's directions. Transfer the sorbet to a covered container and freeze until it is firm enough to scoop, at least 1 hour or overnight. If the sorbet becomes too firm in the freezer, let it sit at room temperature for 5 to 10 minutes before scooping.

Note: To make a puree, process ripe fruit in a blender or food processor until smooth. If time is short, consider store-bought fruit purees, such as unsweetened applesauce. For best results the puree must have body and not be too liquid; it should be thick enough to coat the back of a spoon. (Excess liquid can be removed from a puree by placing it in a coffee filter to drain.) To test, dip a spoon into the puree, then draw your finger across the back of the spoon. The mark left by your finger should remain intact.

70 cal, 0.5 g fat, 0.5 g prot, 15 g carb

- 2 cups fruit juice, such as apple (for light-colored fruits) or cranberry (for darker fruits)
- 2 cups thick fruit puree (see Note), such as mango, pear, papaya, or cantaloupe
- 1 tablespoon vodka or light rum

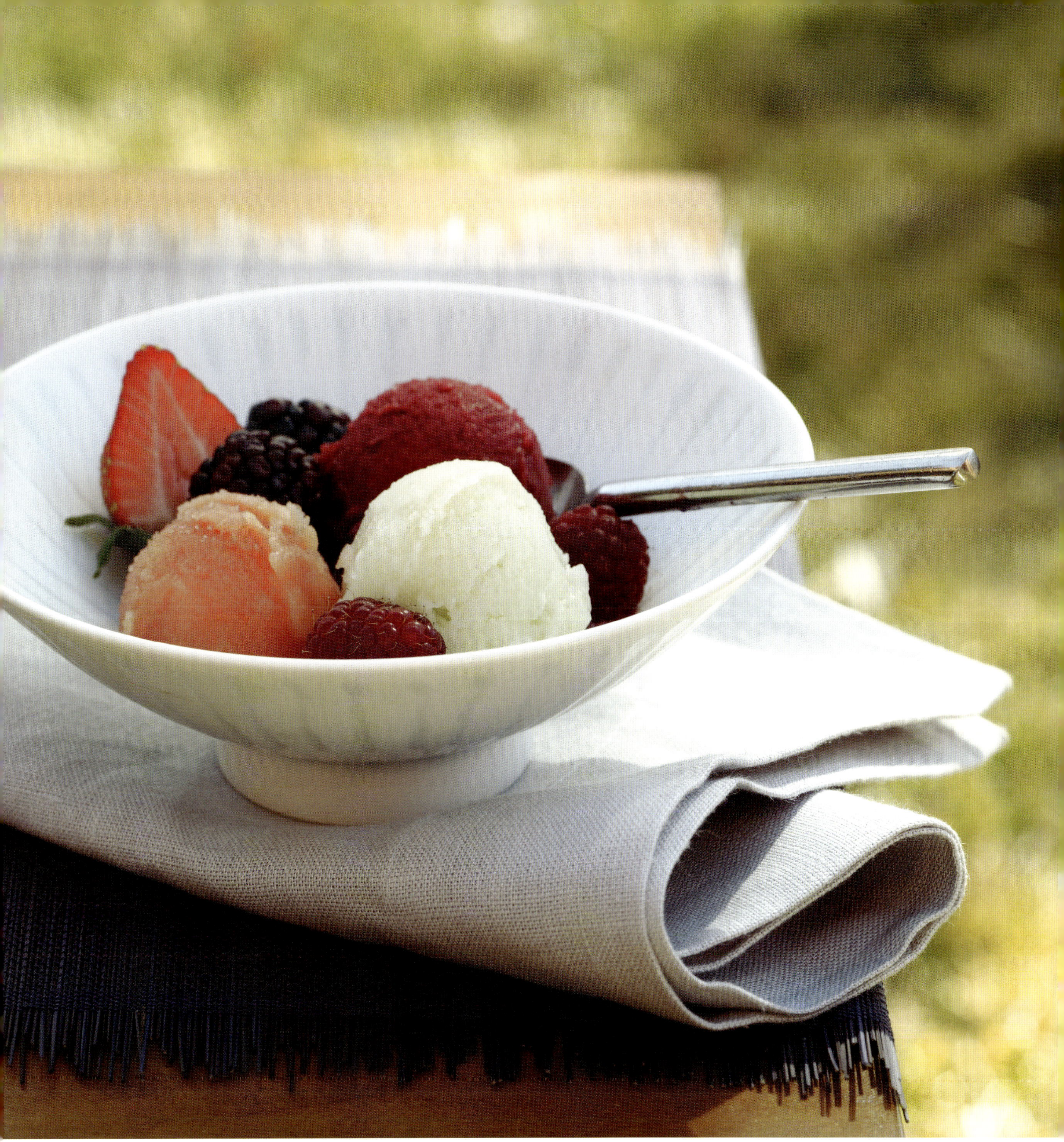

tiramisu

Makes one 13 x 9–inch pan, to serve 24

Tiramisu has become the sweet symbol of America's love affair with Italian food. Because it is normally such an indulgence, our chefs have developed this spectacular dessert that tastes just as decadent as the original, without the guilt. If purchasing egg whites commercially, look for containers of natural egg whites; the pasteurized whites sold in small cartons will not whip.

To make the cake: Preheat the oven to 350°F. Line 2 jelly-roll pans (approximately 15 x 10 x 1 inch) with parchment paper and spray with nonstick cooking spray. In a large bowl, combine the egg whites, sugar, and cream of tartar. Beat with an electric mixer until soft peaks form. Sift the flour over the top and fold it in with a large rubber spatula until just blended. Divide the mixture between the prepared pans, gently spreading it evenly to the edges. Bake, reversing the position of the pans in the oven halfway through, until the top springs back when touched gently with your finger, 25 to 30 minutes. Let cool.

To make the filling: In a large bowl, combine the cream cheese and sugar. Beat with an electric mixer until well blended. Beat in the coffee liqueur, wine, vanilla, and espresso powder.

In another large bowl, using a whisk or clean beaters, whip the whites with the cream of tartar until stiff peaks form. Mix about one fourth of the egg whites into the cheese mixture to lighten it, then fold in the remaining whites.

Cut each sheet of cake in half widthwise. Fit half of 1 of the cakes into a 13 x 9 x 2–inch baking dish or pan. (It's fine if it doesn't fit perfectly.) Spread about one fourth of the cheese filling evenly over the cake. Top with another layer of cake, then filling, and repeat until all the cake has been layered. Spread the remaining filling over the top. Cover and refrigerate for at least 2 hours or overnight to blend the flavors. Sprinkle the top with cocoa powder and cinnamon and, if you wish, a few fresh chocolate shavings. To serve, cut into small squares.

219 cal, 1 g fat, 9 g prot, 28 g carb

» Cake
- 20 large egg whites (about 3⅓ cups)
- 1⅓ cups sugar
- ½ teaspoon cream of tartar
- 1 cup cake flour

» Filling
- 1¾ pounds nonfat cream cheese, at room temperature
- ½ cup sugar
- 1 tablespoon coffee-flavored liqueur, such as Kahlúa
- 1 tablespoon sweet Marsala wine
- 1½ teaspoons vanilla extract
- 1½ teaspoons instant espresso powder
- 7 large egg whites (about 1¼ cups)
- ½ teaspoon cream of tartar

Cocoa powder, for garnish
Ground cinnamon, for garnish
Chocolate shavings, for garnish (optional)

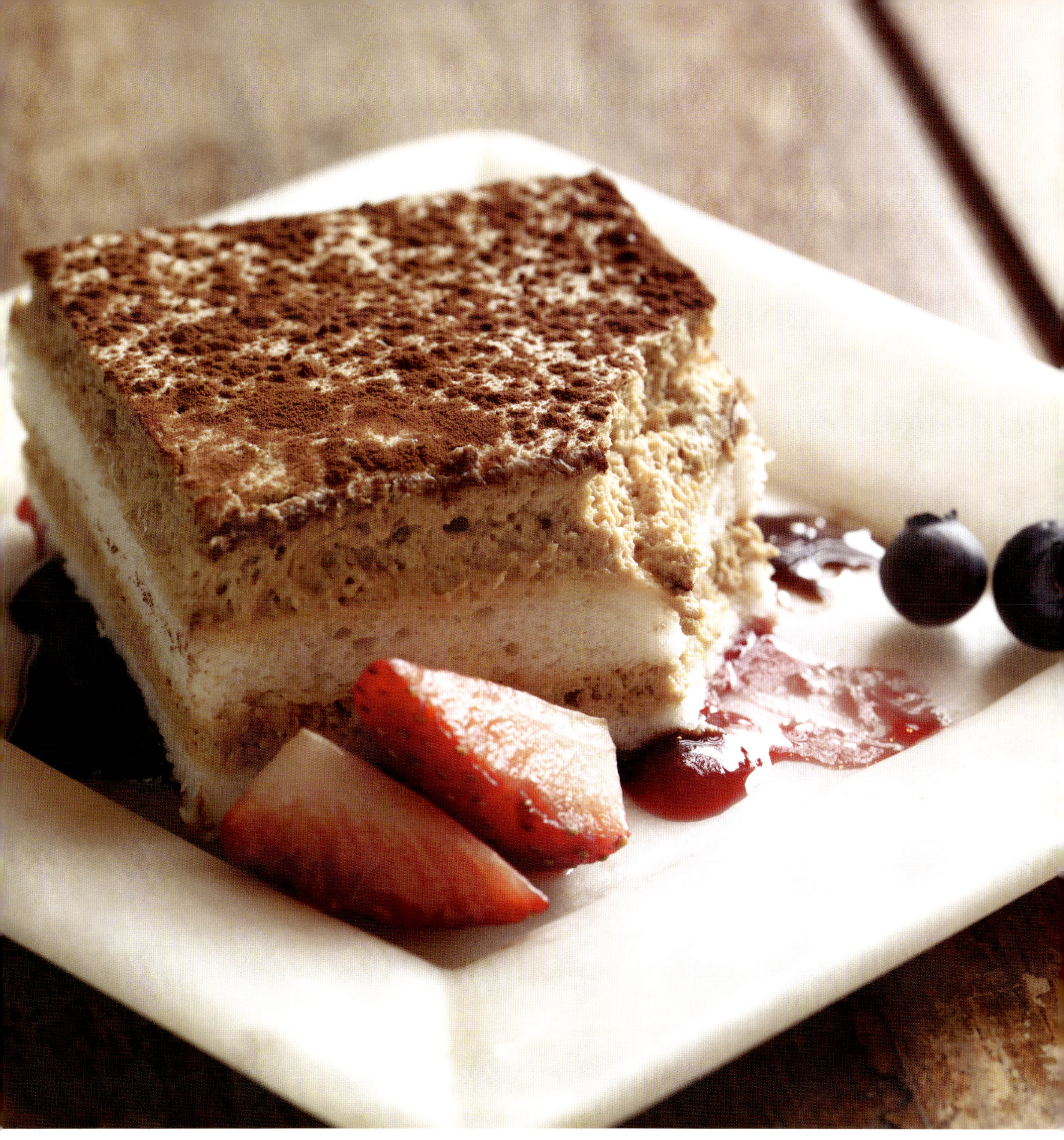

tapioca pudding brûlée

Serves 6

Crème Brûlée is such a favorite with everyone that we've included two versions. This one is a twist on the traditional, based on the tapioca pudding many of us remember from our youth. We caramelize the top and serve it in a ramekin. It has a unique texture because of the fresh tapioca pearls.

Soak the tapioca in about ¾ cup cold water for 10 minutes to soften.

In a heavy medium saucepan, combine the tapioca and water, milk, egg yolk, vanilla, and salt. Cook over medium heat, whisking constantly until thickened, 5 to 7 minutes. Whisk 6 tablespoons of the sugar together with the 2 egg whites until frothy. While whisking, pour some of the hot milk mixture into the egg whites. Scrape the whites and milk back into the milk saucepan. Whisk constantly to prevent scorching, and cook until thick.

Divide the pudding evenly among six 6-ounce flameproof custard cups or ramekins. Refrigerate uncovered until the puddings are cold and set, about 4 hours.

Just before serving, sprinkle 1 teaspoon of sugar evenly over the surface of each cold pudding, covering the top completely. Using a propane or butane kitchen torch, move the flame back and forth, close to the sugar, until it melts and bubbles and then caramelizes and turns golden brown. (Alternatively, preheat the broiler until hot. Place the cold ramekins cups on a baking sheet and broil 6 to 8 inches from the heat, watching carefully, until the sugar is golden brown and caramelized.) Let stand until the sugar has cooled and hardened, 3 to 5 minutes. Serve at once. Each diner should use a spoon to crack the caramelized sugar crust, taking a spoonful of the creamy pudding with each bite, along with a bit of the crust.

149 cal, 1 g fat, 4 g prot, 31 g carb

- ⅓ cup small tapioca pearls
- 2 cups nonfat milk
- 1 large egg, separated
- 1 teaspoon vanilla extract
- 8 tablespoons sugar, divided
- 1 large egg white
- Dash of salt

crème brûlée with fresh berries

Serves 4

This version of the perennial restaurant favorite gets an added burst of flavor and texture with the addition of a few fresh berries. This crème brûlée is made like the classic version, it just uses more egg whites in place of egg yolks and 2 percent milk instead of half-and-half and cream. This cuts out a major amount of calories and thus can be eaten without feeling guilty!

Preheat the oven to 325°F. In a small heavy saucepan, whisk together the milk and the 2½ tablespoons sugar. Use a small sharp knife to cut the vanilla bean in half lengthwise. Use the tip of the knife to scrape the vanilla bean seeds into the milk, then add the halved vanilla bean for extra flavor. Cook over medium heat just until bubbles appear around the edge of the pan.

In a small bowl, whisk together the eggs and egg white. Add about ½ cup of the warm milk mixture, whisking until well blended. Pour back into the saucepan and reduce the heat to low. Cook, stirring, until the mixture is thick enough to coat the back of a spoon, about 3 minutes. Do not let boil. Strain the custard through a sieve to remove any bits of cooked egg.

Place about 3 tablespoons of berries in each of four 6-ounce flameproof ramekins or custard cups. Place the ramekins in a larger roasting pan and add enough hot water to reach halfway up the sides of the ramekins. Divide the custard evenly among the ramekins, about ¼ cup per serving. Bake until the custards are set and a knife inserted into the custard comes out clean, about 30 minutes. Remove the custards from the water bath and let cool.

Refrigerate uncovered until the custards are thoroughly chilled, about 4 hours.

Just before serving, sprinkle 1 teaspoon of sugar evenly over the surface of each cold custard, covering the top completely. Using a propane or butane kitchen torch, move the flame back and forth, close to the sugar, until it melts and bubbles and then caramelizes and turns golden brown. (Alternatively, preheat the broiler until hot. Place the ramekins cups on a baking sheet and broil 6 to 8 inches from the heat, watching carefully, until the sugar is golden brown and caramelized.) Let stand until the sugar has cooled and hardened, 3 to 5 minutes. Serve at once. Each diner should use a spoon to crack the caramelized sugar crust, taking a spoonful of the creamy berry custard with each bite, along with a bit of the crust.

131 cal, 4 g fat, 7 g prot, 16 g carb

1	cup 2 percent low-fat milk
2½	tablespoons sugar, plus 4 teaspoons for topping
½	vanilla bean (2 to 3 inches long)
2	large eggs
1	large egg white
¾	cup fresh blueberries or raspberries

almond ricotta torte

Serves 8

Our chefs bake these Italian-style tortes in tiny silicone molds, which give the exterior a smooth texture and make unmolding a breeze. If you have one, a silicone cupcake pan would also work here; otherwise, bake these in 4-ounce ramekins that have been coated with nonstick cooking spray. Serve with fresh berries.

Preheat the oven to 325°F. In a large bowl, stir together the sugar, almonds, graham cracker crumbs, and flour. Mix in the ricotta, egg yolk, vanilla extract, almond extract, and lemon zest.

In another large bowl, using a whisk or electric mixer, beat the 2 egg whites until medium peaks form. Fold about one fourth of the egg whites into the ricotta mixture to lighten it, then fold in the remaining whites. Place eight 3- to 4-ounce molds on a baking sheet. Using a ⅓-cup measure, divide the mixture equally among the molds. Bake until a knife inserted into the center of the tortes comes out clean, about 20 minutes. Let cool completely.

If using silicone molds, unmold onto individual dessert plates. For ramekins, unmold onto a plate or serve directly from the ramekin. The tortes can be made up to 1 day in advance and refrigerated, covered. Serve slightly chilled, garnished with fresh berries.

104 cal, 2 g fat, 5 g prot, 14 g carb

- 3 tablespoons sugar
- 2½ tablespoons toasted ground almonds
- 2½ tablespoons graham cracker crumbs
- 1½ tablespoons all-purpose flour
- 1 cup nonfat ricotta cheese
- 1 large egg, separated
- ½ teaspoon vanilla extract
- ⅛ teaspoon almond extract
- 1 large egg white

Finely grated zest of ½ lemon (about 1 teaspoon)

Fresh berries, for garnish

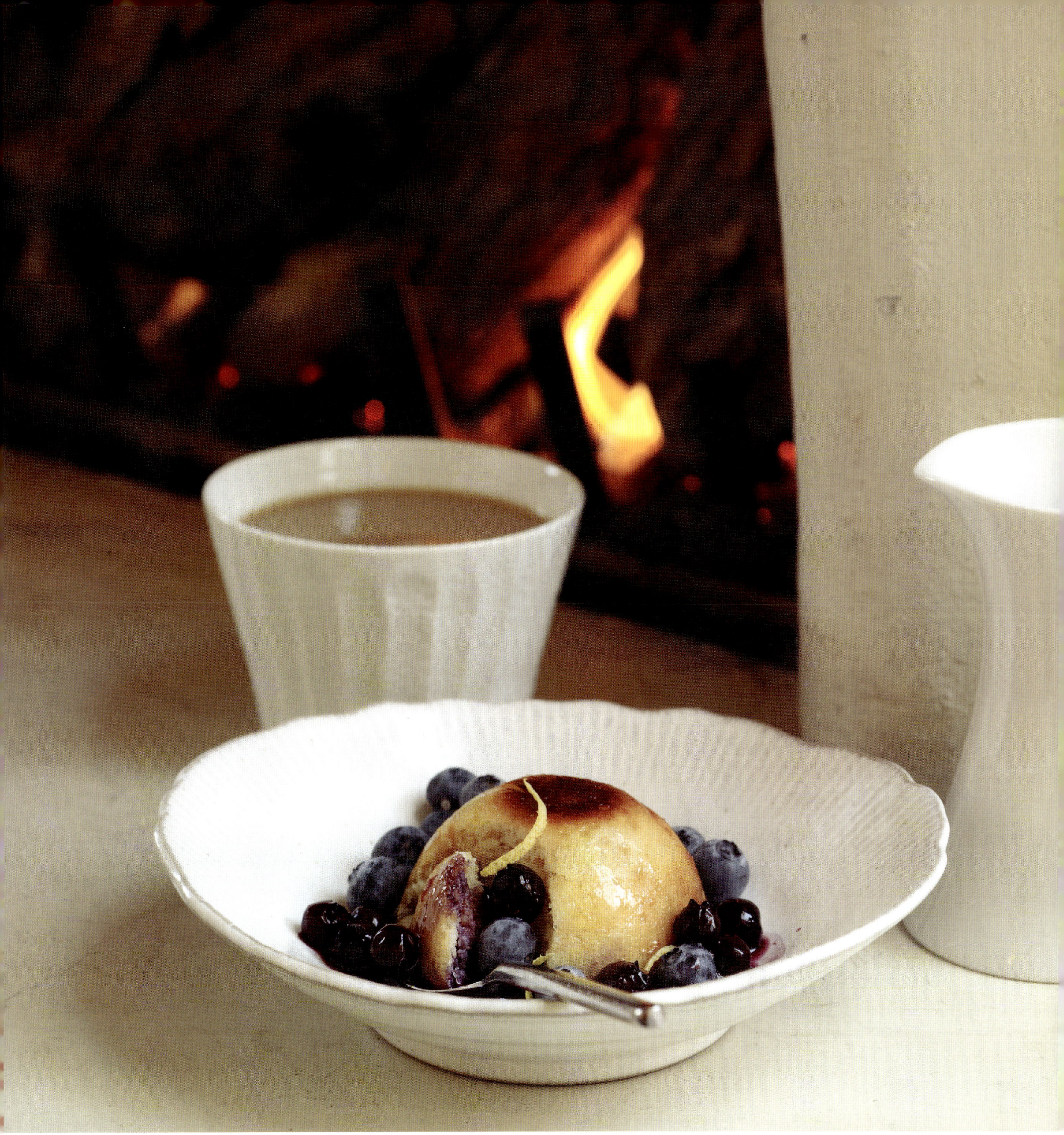

chocolate chip cheesecake

Makes one 9- or 10-inch cheesecake, to serve 20

Cheesecake is always one of our most popular desserts, but an added touch of chocolate sends this one over the top. Best of all, this party-sized cheesecake comes together quickly with a food processor and can be made well in advance.

Preheat the oven to 325°F. Spray a 9- or 10-inch springform pan with a removable bottom with nonstick cooking spray, and wrap the outside with a double thickness of aluminum foil to prevent leakage. In a medium bowl, mix together the graham cracker crumbs and melted butter until evenly moistened. Press the crumb mixture evenly onto the bottom of the prepared springform pan.

In a food processor, puree the cottage cheese until smooth. Add the cream cheese and sugar and process until well blended.

In a glass measuring cup, whisk together the egg whites, egg, vanilla, lemon juice, and salt until blended. With the processor running, gradually add the egg mixture to the cheese until just blended; do not overmix. Add the chocolate chips, pulsing the machine on and off 2 or 3 times, until just blended.

Pour the batter into the springform pan, then place it inside a larger roasting pan or other shallow baking dish. Add enough hot water to the roasting pan to reach halfway up the sides of the springform. Bake until the top of the cheesecake is firm at the edges and just barely set in the center, 55 to 60 minutes. Carefully remove the pans from the oven and place on a wire rack. Let the cheesecake cool to room temperature in the water bath. Remove it from the water bath and cover with plastic wrap. Refrigerate until thoroughly chilled, at least 4 hours or overnight.

Run a blunt knife around the edge of the pan to loosen, then release the springform. To serve, cut into thin wedges.

177 cal, 5 g fat, 8 g prot, 23 g carb

- 1 cup graham cracker crumbs
- 2 tablespoons unsalted butter, melted
- 3 cups low-fat cottage cheese
- 1½ cups (12 ounces) nonfat cream cheese, at room temperature
- 1 cup sugar
- 4 large egg whites (about ⅔ cup)
- 1 large egg
- 4 teaspoons vanilla extract
- 2 teaspoons fresh lemon juice
- ½ teaspoon salt
- 1 cup (6 ounces) semisweet chocolate chips

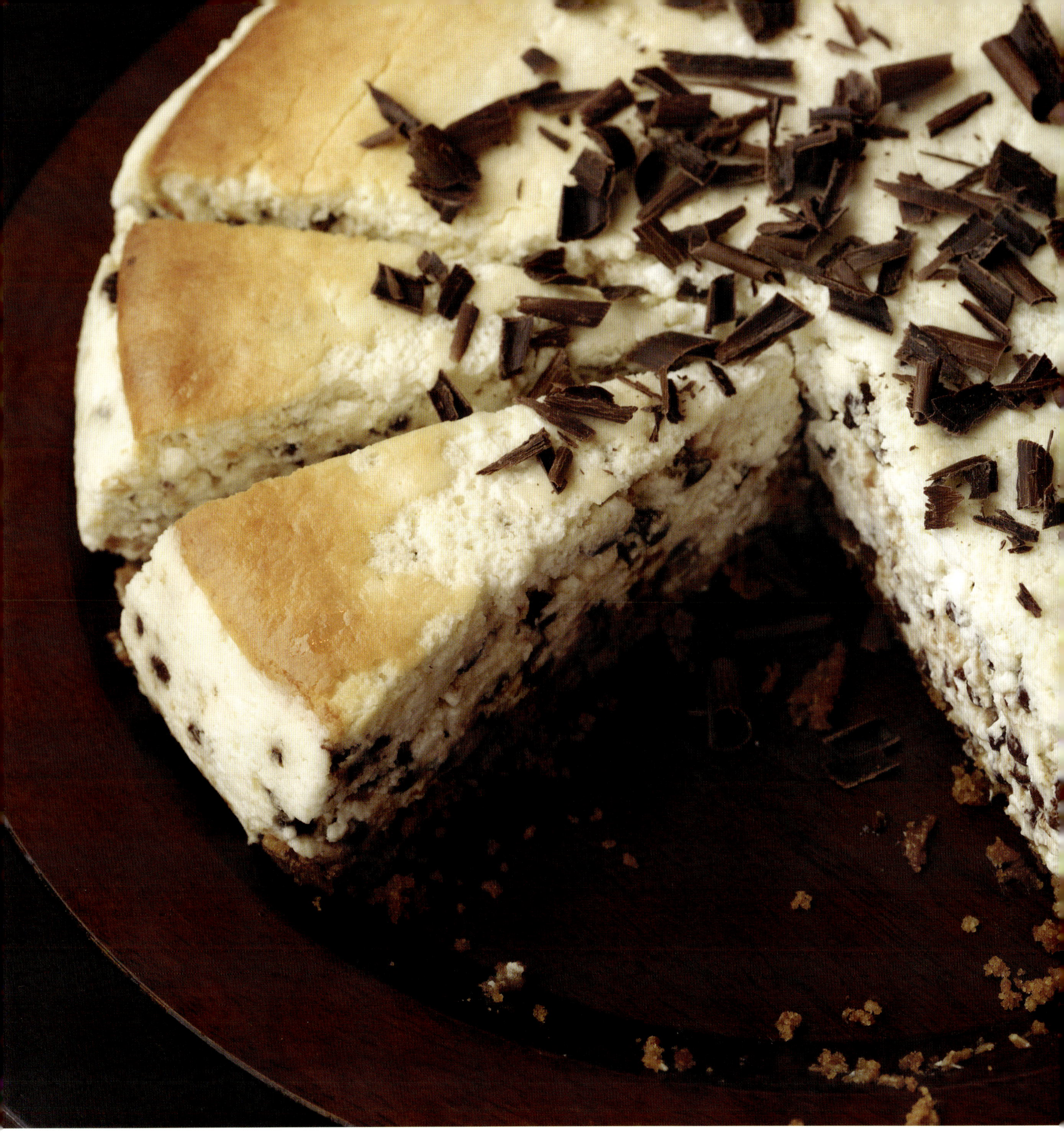

suggested menus
breakfast

/p. 30   Mii amo Passage Smoothie
/p. 42   Tofu Scramble
/p. 50   Carrot-Bran Muffins

/p. 40   Egg White Omelet with roasted potatoes
/p. 51   Cranberry-Orange Bread with fresh fruit in season

/p. 37   Berry Yogurt Parfait with Granola
/p. 44   Cinnamon French Toast

/p. 34   Berry Temptress Smoothie
/p. 47   Blue Corn Waffles with Dried Fruit Compote

/p. 32   Mayan Breeze Smoothie
/p. 35   Blueberry Muffins
/p. 39   Apple Cottage Griddle Cakes

lunch

/p. 68	Vegetarian Chili
/p. 71	Chicken Napoleon with Cabernet Jus
/p. 124	Fruit Sorbet

/p. 65	Crab Spring Rolls with Mango-Chile Dipping Sauce
/p. 76	Whole Wheat–Honey Flatbread with Prosciutto and Three-Herb Pesto
/p. 120	Fresh Fruit Tart

/p. 56	Asian Chicken Salad with Miso-Mango Vinaigrette
/p. 61	Salmon and Spinach Risotto with Red Wine Glaze
/p. 128	Tapioca Pudding Brûlée

/p. 54	Tomato Gazpacho
/p. 73	Veggie Burger with Sweet Onion Ketchup
/p. 118	Berry Martini

/p. 59	Pan-Seared Ahi Tuna with Cellophane Noodles and Red Curry Broth
/p. 132	Chocolate Chip Cheesecake

dinner

/p. 94   Onion Soup
/p. 110 Filet Mignon with Truffled Peruvian Potatoes and Wild Mushroom Demi-Glace
/p. 126 Tiramisu

/p. 88   Baby Beet Salad with Tart Cherry Vinaigrette
/p. 104 Grilled Sea Bass with Orzo Primavera and Saffron Broth
/p. 129 Crème Brûlée with Fresh Berries

/p. 96   Crab and Corn Cakes with Rémoulade Sauce
/p. 107 Herb-Crusted Colorado Lamb with Rosemary Jus
/p. 130 Almond Ricotta Torte

/p. 91   Arugula and Tomato Salad with Basil Vinaigrette and Balsamic Syrup
/p. 100 Grilled Salmon with Yukon Gold Potato Tart and Asparagus-Asiago Cream
/p. 122 Cherry-Apple Strudel

/p. 99   Shrimp Sauté with Orzo and Vegetables
/p. 112 Buffalo Tenderloin with Horseradish Potato Cake and Chipotle-Tomato Jus
/p. 119 Peach-Blueberry Crisp

Steve Bernstein (right), executive chef of Enchantment Resort and Mii amo Spa, and Steve Sicinski (left), spa chef of Mii amo Spa

"To me, there's only one way to cook: Use the highest quality, freshest, and most natural ingredients, and know the source. Cut back on fat and cholesterol, eliminate butter and cream, and control portion size. Think of a portion as four ounces protein, more vegetables and grains. It's a healthier approach to classic cuisine. And do make time to sit down and enjoy three meals a day."

» Executive Chef Steve Bernstein

"Mii amo is a luxury-oriented spa, and we cater to our guests with a fine-dining experience, which is really a reeducation about how to eat and be satisfied without stuffing yourself. We can give you a three-course meal for under 700 calories. I call it intelligent cuisine. I want to give you what you want and what you like, but with fewer calories. I don't want you to sacrifice. Let me worry about the calories and fat."

» Spa Chef Steve Sicinski

Index

A

Almond Ricotta Torte, 130
Apples
    Apple Cottage Griddle Cakes, 39
    Cherry-Apple Strudel, 122
Artichokes
    Artichoke Spread, 82
    Warm Crab Spread, 84
Arugula and Tomato Salad with Basil Vinaigrette and Balsamic Syrup, 91
Asian Chicken Salad with Miso-Mango Vinaigrette, 56
Asparagus
    Asparagus-Asiago Cream, 103
    Baby Beet Salad with Tart Cherry Vinaigrette, 88
    Chicken Napoleon with Cabernet Jus, 71

B

Baby Beet Salad with Tart Cherry Vinaigrette, 88
Balsamic Syrup, 93
Bananas
    Berry Temptress Smoothie, 34
    Fresh Fruit Tart, 120
    Mayan Breeze Smoothie, 32
    Mii amo Passage Smoothie, 30
Basil Vinaigrette, 92
Beans
    Herb-Crusted Colorado Lamb with Rosemary Jus, 107
    Hummus, 86
    Shrimp Sauté with Orzo and Vegetables, 99
    Tuscan White Bean Spread, 83
    Vegetarian Chili, 68
Beef
    Filet Mignon with Truffled Peruvian Potatoes and Wild Mushroom Demi-Glace, 110
Beet Salad, Baby, with Tart Cherry Vinaigrette, 88
Bell peppers
    Chicken Napoleon with Cabernet Jus, 71
    Roasted Eggplant and Red Pepper Spread, 87
    Tomato Gazpacho, 54
    Veggie Burger with Sweet Onion Ketchup, 73
    Warm Crab Spread, 84
Berries
    Berry Martini, 118
    Berry Temptress Smoothie, 34
    Berry Yogurt Parfait with Granola, 37
    Blueberry Muffins, 35
    Cinnamon French Toast, 44
    Cranberry-Orange Bread, 51
    Crème Brûlée with Fresh Berries, 129
    Fresh Fruit Tart, 120
    Granola, 38
    Mayan Breeze Smoothie, 32
    Mii amo Passage Smoothie, 30
    Peach-Blueberry Crisp, 119
Blackberries
    Berry Temptress Smoothie, 34
    Fresh Fruit Tart, 120
    Mayan Breeze Smoothie, 32
Blueberries
    Berry Martini, 118
    Berry Temptress Smoothie, 34
    Berry Yogurt Parfait with Granola, 37
    Blueberry Muffins, 35
    Crème Brûlée with Fresh Berries, 129
    Fresh Fruit Tart, 120
    Peach-Blueberry Crisp, 119
Blue Corn Waffle Mix, 48
Blue Corn Waffles with Dried Fruit Compote, 47
Bok choy
    Asian Chicken Salad with Miso-Mango Vinaigrette, 56
Bran
    Carrot-Bran Muffins, 50
    Cranberry-Orange Bread, 51
Bread
    Cinnamon French Toast, 44
    Cranberry-Orange Bread, 51
    Whole Wheat–Honey Flatbread with Prosciutto and Three-Herb Pesto, 76
Broths. *See* Stocks and broths
Buffalo Tenderloin with Horseradish Potato Cake and Chipotle-Tomato Jus, 112
Burger, Veggie, with Sweet Onion Ketchup, 73

C

Cabbage
    Asian Chicken Salad with Miso-Mango Vinaigrette, 56
Cabernet Jus, 72
Cantaloupe
    Fruit Sorbet, 124
Carrots
    Carrot-Bran Muffins, 50
    Crab Spring Rolls with Mango-Chile Dipping Sauce, 65
    Veggie Burger with Sweet Onion Ketchup, 73
Cheese
    Almond Ricotta Torte, 130
    Apple Cottage Griddle Cakes, 39
    Artichoke Spread, 82
    Arugula and Tomato Salad with Basil Vinaigrette and Balsamic Syrup, 91

Asparagus-Asiago Cream, 103
Chicken Napoleon with Cabernet Jus, 71
Chocolate Chip Cheesecake, 132
Mii amo Cream Sauce, 85
Tiramisu, 126
Warm Crab Spread, 84
Cherries
　Cherry-Apple Strudel, 122
　Tart Cherry Vinaigrette, 90
Chicken
　Asian Chicken Salad with Miso-Mango Vinaigrette, 56
　Chicken Napoleon with Cabernet Jus, 71
Chili, Vegetarian, 68
Chipotle-Tomato Jus, 114
Chocolate Chip Cheesecake, 132
Cinnamon French Toast, 44
Coffee
　Tiramisu, 126
Compote, Dried Fruit, 49
Cornmeal
　Blue Corn Waffle Mix, 48
　Blue Corn Waffles, 47
　Crab and Corn Cakes with Rémoulade Sauce, 96
Crab
　Crab and Corn Cakes with Rémoulade Sauce, 96
　Crab Spring Rolls with Mango-Chile Dipping Sauce, 65
　Warm Crab Spread, 84
Cranberries
　Cranberry-Orange Bread, 51
　Granola, 38
Crème Brûlée with Fresh Berries, 129
Crisp, Peach-Blueberry, 119
Crystal Grotto, 12, 16
Cucumbers
　Asian Chicken Salad with Miso-Mango Vinaigrette, 56
　Tomato Gazpacho, 54
Currants
　Granola, 38

D

Desserts
　Almond Ricotta Torte, 130
　Berry Martini, 118
　Cherry-Apple Strudel, 122
　Chocolate Chip Cheesecake, 132
　Crème Brûlée with Fresh Berries, 129
　Fresh Fruit Tart, 120
　Fruit Sorbet, 124
　Peach-Blueberry Crisp, 119
　Tapioca Pudding Brûlée, 128
　Tiramisu, 126
Dried Fruit Compote, 49

E

Eggplant
　Roasted Eggplant and Red Pepper Spread, 87
　Vegetarian Chili, 68
Egg White Omelet, 40

Enchantment Resort, 10

F

Filet Mignon with Truffled Peruvian Potatoes and Wild Mushroom Demi-Glace, 110
Fish
　Grilled Salmon with Yukon Gold Potato Tart and Asparagus-Asiago Cream, 100
　Grilled Sea Bass with Orzo Primavera and Saffron Broth, 104
　Pan-Seared Ahi Tuna with Cellophane Noodles and Red Curry Broth, 59
　Salmon and Spinach Risotto with Red Wine Glaze, 61
Flax seeds
　Blueberry Muffins, 35
French Toast, Cinnamon, 44
Fresh Fruit Tart, 120
Fruit. *See also individual fruits*
　Dried Fruit Compote, 49
　Fresh Fruit Tart, 120
　Fruit Sorbet, 124

G

Garlic, Roasted, 78
Gazpacho, Tomato, 54
Glaze, Red Wine, 62
Granola, 38
Griddle Cakes, Apple Cottage, 39
Grilled Salmon with Yukon Gold Potato Tart and Asparagus-Asiago Cream, 100
Grilled Sea Bass with Orzo Primavera and Saffron Broth, 104

H

Herb-Crusted Colorado Lamb with Rosemary Jus, 107
Hummus, 86

J

Jus
　Cabernet Jus, 72
　Chipotle-Tomato Jus, 114
　Rosemary Jus, 108

K

Ketchup, Sweet Onion, 74

L

Lamb, Herb-Crusted Colorado, with Rosemary Jus, 107

M

Mangoes
　Asian Chicken Salad with Miso-Mango Vinaigrette, 56
　Fruit Sorbet, 124
　Mango-Chile Dipping Sauce, 66

Miso-Mango Vinaigrette, 57
Mayan Breeze Smoothie, 32
Menus, suggested, 135–37
Mii amo
    experience of, 9–10, 12, 15–20
    food of, 12, 24–26
    layout of, 10, 12, 24
    location of, 9, 10
    meaning of, 9
    opening of, 9
Mii amo Cream Sauce, 85
Mii amo Passage Smoothie, 30
Miso-Mango Vinaigrette, 57
Muffins
    Blueberry Muffins, 35
    Carrot-Bran Muffins, 50
Mushrooms
    Cabernet Jus, 72
    Egg White Omelet, 40
    Saffron Broth, 106
    Tofu Scramble, 42
    Veggie Burger with Sweet Onion Ketchup, 73
    Wild Mushroom Demi-Glace, 111

N

Nectarines
    Fresh Fruit Tart, 120
Noodles. See Pasta and noodles

O

Oats
    Granola, 38
    Peach-Blueberry Crisp, 119
    Veggie Burger with Sweet Onion Ketchup, 73
Omelet, Egg White, 40
Onions
    Onion Soup, 94
    Sweet Onion Ketchup, 74

P

Pan-Seared Ahi Tuna with Cellophane Noodles and Red Curry Broth, 59
Papayas
    Fruit Sorbet, 124
Parfait, Berry Yogurt, with Granola, 37
Pasta and noodles
    Grilled Sea Bass with Orzo Primavera and Saffron Broth, 104
    Pan-Seared Ahi Tuna with Cellophane Noodles and Red Curry Broth, 59
    Shrimp Sauté with Orzo and Vegetables, 99
Peaches
    Fresh Fruit Tart, 120
    Peach-Blueberry Crisp, 119
Pears
    Fruit Sorbet, 124

Pesto, Three-Herb, 77
Phyllo dough
    Cherry-Apple Strudel, 122
Potatoes
    Buffalo Tenderloin with Horseradish Potato Cake and Chipotle-Tomato Jus, 112
    Filet Mignon with Truffled Peruvian Potatoes and Wild Mushroom Demi-Glace, 110
    Yukon Gold Potato Tart, 102
Prosciutto
    Whole Wheat–Honey Flatbread with Prosciutto and Three-Herb Pesto, 76
    Yukon Gold Potato Tart, 102
Pudding Brûlée, Tapioca, 128
Pumpkin seeds
    Granola, 38

Q

Quinoa
    Veggie Burger with Sweet Onion Ketchup, 73

R

Raspberries
    Berry Martini, 118
    Berry Temptress Smoothie, 34
    Berry Yogurt Parfait with Granola, 37
    Crème Brûlée with Fresh Berries, 129
    Fresh Fruit Tart, 120
Red Curry Broth, 60
Red Wine Glaze, 62
Rémoulade Sauce, 98
Risotto, Salmon and Spinach, with Red Wine Glaze, 61
Roasted Eggplant and Red Pepper Spread, 87
Roasted Garlic, 78
Rosemary Jus, 108

S

Saffron Broth, 106
Salads
    Arugula and Tomato Salad with Basil Vinaigrette and Balsamic Syrup, 91
    Asian Chicken Salad with Miso-Mango Vinaigrette, 56
    Baby Beet Salad with Tart Cherry Vinaigrette, 88
Salmon
    Grilled Salmon with Yukon Gold Potato Tart and Asparagus-Asiago Cream, 100
    Salmon and Spinach Risotto with Red Wine Glaze, 61
Sauces
    Asparagus-Asiago Cream, 103
    Mango-Chile Dipping Sauce, 66
    Mii amo Cream Sauce, 85
    Rémoulade Sauce, 98
    Three-Herb Pesto, 77
    Wild Mushroom Demi-Glace, 111
Sea Bass, Grilled, with Orzo Primavera and Saffron Broth, 104

Shrimp Sauté with Orzo and Vegetables, 99
Smoothies
    Berry Temptress Smoothie, 34
    Mayan Breeze Smoothie, 32
    Mii amo Passage Smoothie, 30
Sorbet, Fruit, 124
Soups
    Onion Soup, 94
    Tomato Gazpacho, 54
Spinach
    Baby Beet Salad with Tart Cherry Vinaigrette, 88
    Egg White Omelet, 40
    Herb-Crusted Colorado Lamb with Rosemary Jus, 107
    Salmon and Spinach Risotto with Red Wine Glaze, 61
    Yukon Gold Potato Tart, 102
Spreads
    Artichoke Spread, 82
    Hummus, 86
    Roasted Eggplant and Red Pepper Spread, 87
    Tuscan White Bean Spread, 83
    Warm Crab Spread, 84
Squash
    Veggie Burger with Sweet Onion Ketchup, 73
Stocks and broths
    Red Curry Broth, 60
    Saffron Broth, 106
    Thickened Vegetable Stock, 79
    Vegetable Stock, 63
Strawberries
    Berry Martini, 118
    Berry Temptress Smoothie, 34
    Berry Yogurt Parfait with Granola, 37
    Fresh Fruit Tart, 120
    Mii amo Passage Smoothie, 30
Strudel, Cherry-Apple, 122
Sunflower seeds
    Granola, 38
Sweet Onion Ketchup, 74
Syrup, Balsamic, 93

T

Tapioca Pudding Brûlée, 128
Tart Cherry Vinaigrette, 90
Tarts
    Fresh Fruit Tart, 120
    Yukon Gold Potato Tart, 102
Tasso
    Chicken Napoleon with Cabernet Jus, 71
    Shrimp Sauté with Orzo and Vegetables, 99
Tea, 27
Thickened Vegetable Stock, 79
Three-Herb Pesto, 77
Tiramisu, 126
Tofu Scramble, 42
Tomatoes
    Arugula and Tomato Salad with Basil Vinaigrette and Balsamic Syrup, 91
    Chipotle-Tomato Jus, 114

Sweet Onion Ketchup, 74
Tomato Gazpacho, 54
Vegetarian Chili, 68
Whole Wheat–Honey Flatbread with Prosciutto and Three-Herb Pesto, 76
Torte, Almond Ricotta, 130
Tuna, Pan-Seared Ahi, with Cellophane Noodles and Red Curry Broth, 59
Tuscan White Bean Spread, 83

V

Vegetables. *See also individual vegetables*
    Shrimp Sauté with Orzo and Vegetables, 99
    Thickened Vegetable Stock, 79
    Vegetable Stock, 63
    Vegetarian Chili, 68
    Veggie Burger with Sweet Onion Ketchup, 73
Vinaigrettes
    Basil Vinaigrette, 92
    Miso-Mango Vinaigrette, 57
    Tart Cherry Vinaigrette, 90

W

Waffles
    Blue Corn Waffle Mix, 48
    Blue Corn Waffles with Dried Fruit Compote, 47
Warm Crab Spread, 84
Whole Wheat–Honey Flatbread with Prosciutto and Three-Herb Pesto, 76
Wild Mushroom Demi-Glace, 111
Wine
    Cabernet Jus, 72
    Red Wine Glaze, 62

Y

Yogurt
    Berry Martini, 118
    Berry Yogurt Parfait with Granola, 37
Yukon Gold Potato Tart, 102

Z

Zucchini
    Veggie Burger with Sweet Onion Ketchup, 73

Table of Equivalents

The exact equivalents in the following tables have been rounded for convenience.

Liquid/Dry Measures

U.S.		Metric	
¼	teaspoon	1.25	milliliters
½	teaspoon	2.5	milliliters
1	teaspoon	5	milliliters
1	tablespoon (3 teaspoons)	15	milliliters
1	fluid ounce (2 tablespoons)	30	milliliters
¼	cup	60	milliliters
⅓	cup	80	milliliters
½	cup	120	milliliters
1	cup	240	milliliters
1	pint (2 cups)	480	milliliters
1	quart (4 cups, 32 ounces)	960	milliliters
1	gallon (4 quarts)	3.84	liters
1	ounce (by weight)	28	grams
1	pound	454	grams
2.2	pounds	1	kilogram

Length

U.S.		Metric	
⅛	inch	3	millimeters
¼	inch	6	millimeters
½	inch	12	millimeters
1	inch	2.5	centimeters

Oven Temperature

Fahrenheit	Celsius	Gas
250	120	½
275	140	1
300	150	2
325	160	3
350	180	4
375	190	5
400	200	6
425	220	7
450	230	8
475	240	9
500	260	10